Sawdust On His Shirt

Rediscovering Jesus

Sawdust On His Shirt

Rediscovering Jesus

Roger Speare

Circle Books

Winchester, UK
Washington, USA

First published by Circle Books, 2014
Circle Books is an imprint of John Hunt Publishing Ltd., Laurel House, Station Approach,
Alresford, Hants, SO24 9JH, UK
office1@jhpbooks.net
www.johnhuntpublishing.com
www.circle-books.com

For distributor details and how to order please visit the 'Ordering' section on our website.

ISBN: 978 1 78279 372 4
Library of Congress Control Number: 2014945522

A CIP catalogue record for this book is available from the British Library.

Design: Stuart Davies

Printed in the USA by Edwards Brothers Malloy

Unless otherwise stated biblical quotations
are from the New King James version.

CONTENTS

Preface

I did not set out to publish a book but as I wrestled with a number of questions that I thought I had answered decades earlier I found myself writing stuff down. In doing so I came to believe that there is an important job waiting to be done by a bunch of people scattered across this planet. If I am right about this then others will probably be thinking and feeling similar things to me. They will have a gnawing hunger for God that they know will never abate until they are firmly bonded with kindred spirits in a network of friendship and prayer that embraces the earth.

If that strikes a chord with you then I think you should read this book.

On the road to reaching that conclusion, however, I found myself needing to examine and to try to understand Jesus' gospel of the kingdom of heaven. What emerged was, at least for me, a fresh view of Jesus and his message. Not only did I start to get a handle on some answers to my questions but it turned out that Jesus is much more inclusive in his thinking and teaching than I had previously thought. And that really is good news.

So if you feel that Jesus may have something important to say to the world but you do not see yourself as ever being a religious person and perhaps you struggle with ideas like the Resurrection and the divinity of Christ then you also might benefit from reading this book. It seems to me that Jesus has made room for you.

We could call these two groups, standing at opposite ends of a spectrum of spirituality, the prophetic intercessors and the skeptical sympathizers. Within the spectrum are many who, like myself, are committed disciples of Jesus Christ. We are seeking a deeper understanding and experience of God and his power and purposes in a troubled world. This book explores the journey into a better future for the human race that Jesus invites all of us to make. If you are still not sure whether it is for you then you may find the Executive Summary helpful.

I am not much of a scholar but there is a fair bit of biblical analysis involved. Much of it is in the notes and appendices but some is necessarily in the body of the text. You will need to approach the Bible with an open mind, willing to take its words seriously and, when appropriate, literally. On the other hand the God I have been getting to know these past sixty years has a wonderful sense of humor and usually allows me to tackle theology with a bit of fun. So if you do decide to read my book – the book that I never intended to write – there is a good chance you will find it fairly easy on the mind. You might be shocked or entertained or challenged but I hope you will enjoy it and find in it some food for thought. You are welcome to let me know if (when, more likely) you spot my mistakes.

Roger Speare
sawdustonhisshirt@gmail.com

Executive Summary

1 Gazebos for God

Even some people who met the risen Jesus did not believe in his resurrection. It is, therefore, not surprising that the gospel Jesus preached allows for honest doubt. His key themes are actually "repentance" and "childlikeness". So, starting from an atheistic view of spirituality we examine the implications of Jesus' gospel for those who do not believe in God and how believers should relate to them.

2 Mary's Story

Continuing our search for the essence of Jesus' gospel we consider the case for the joined-up version of Mary of Bethany's story to be the essential accompaniment to the gospel of Jesus. By retelling the story we help to propagate it afresh in the third millennium.

3 Spikenard Love

It emerges from Mary's story that the most fundamental aspect of the character of God, and therefore of Jesus' gospel, is love. Love has a two-way cause-effect relationship with forgiveness, which in turn is closely associated with healing. Faith starts to emerge from our examination of this spiritual dynamic.

4 Second Childhood

We continue unpacking faith, drawing on the personality, experience and teaching of Jesus. We show that each of us needs to rediscover childlike dependence on our heavenly Father in order to reverse the effects of the Fall, develop real wisdom and find a pathway to healing and service.

5 Renewed Minds

In this chapter we address the work of the Holy Spirit and the example of Jesus in enabling us to get free from sub-optimal behavior. Repentance takes on multiple dimensions. Lifetime goals come into focus. We tackle the question of how we can actually "be perfect, just as our Father in heaven is perfect". And we take a look at the Cross in the light of these ideas.

6 Spiritual Warfare

We then turn our attention to spiritual warfare, the other main aspect of the work of the Holy Spirit. We discover how the Spirit enables us to become active in the battle to defeat evil and extend goodness in our world. We examine the nature of demons and angels and think about the problem of pain and suffering. And we establish the importance of the Bible.

7 Your Kingdom Come

Taking the warfare theme forward we study the Lord's Prayer. We consider the nature of the kingdom of God. We enter the holy ground of worship, explore God's call for prophetic intercessors and survey the kind of training process they will need to go through in order to fulfill that role.

8 The House of Prayer

In this chapter we consider the corporate dimension of Christianity and Jesus' intention for the church to be a house of prayer for all nations, the spiritual temple at the heart of the kingdom. We examine Jesus' mental picture of his church as a building and discover the importance of harmonious relationships therein. We pin down the important distinction between the kingdom of God and the church.

9 Leavening the Lump

Yeast, another of Jesus' pictures of his church, combines effectively with his building model and the Old Testament Tabernacle. We note how these three models reveal a path of individual progress into greater levels of spiritual authority and we begin to get a sense of where Jesus is leading his church.

10 Mysterious Symmetries

The eight parables of Easter week provide the framework for a study of Jesus' teaching about the end of the age and the consummation of the kingdom. We face the fact that Jesus really did foresee a cataclysmic supernatural change in the nature of reality. We identify the relationship of that event to the present period of human history and touch on the scientific potential for such a change.

11 The Day of the Lord

We note how God's interaction with humanity has been tidal or seasonal in nature, periods of spiritual renewal being followed by decline as God, with endless patience, recycles human cock-ups. Yet overall there has been progress. We identify the challenge for Christians living today to seize a unique opportunity as the tide rises again.

Chapter 1

Gazebos for God

I have this recurrent daydream about the Father, Son and Holy Spirit at a board meeting in heaven when there was only them and nothing else existed. They are planning the universe and they have worked their way through the agenda from the big bang and all that was to follow it until they have reached the Incarnation: God is to become human. The Father and the Son have been discussing this with great enthusiasm and excitement while the Holy Spirit has been quietly listening. Finally the Holy Spirit speaks: "You know what's going to happen?" The Father and Son pay attention. "They will make a religion out of it." The Son looks at the Father and says: "She's right." [1] With a grateful smile in the direction of the Holy Spirit the Father nods his agreement. "We will need a contingency plan", he says.

It will come as no surprise that I hardly ever find myself agreeing with atheist philosophers. However, coming across Daniel Dennett's book, *Breaking the Spell*, turned out to be one of those rare occasions. In *Breaking the Spell* Dennett deals with "religion as a natural phenomenon", arguing that religion is a human invention. I think he is correct. The apostle Peter unwittingly demonstrated this human inventiveness on a mountaintop one day when he saw Jesus' face dramatically change to shine like the sun, saw his clothes become an intense white and saw him chatting with Moses and Elijah, two long-dead prophets back on a day trip from Paradise. And the best Peter could come up with as a response was, "Hey, Jesus, I'd really like to build three gazebos for you guys." That is religion – a well meaning but bumbling and in the end futile attempt to capture and preserve the essence of an encounter with The Numinous.

In the course of debunking religion, however, Dennett comes

up against the awkward phenomenon of spirituality. He realizes that spirituality is quite distinct from religion – people can be spiritual without being religious, and vice versa – and that spirituality is too big a deal to be ignored. It is a whole different ballgame from religion. So he has to find a way to fit spirituality into his analysis and the following passage represents his best shot at doing that.

> *Let your self go. If you can approach the world's complexities, both its glories and its horrors, with an attitude of humble curiosity, acknowledging that however deeply you have seen, you have only just scratched the surface, you will find worlds within worlds, beauties you could not heretofore imagine, and your own mundane preoccupations will shrink to proper size, not all that important in the greater scheme of things. Keeping that awestruck vision of the world ready to hand while dealing with the demands of daily living is no easy exercise, but it is definitely worth the effort, for if you can stay centered, and engaged, you will find the hard choices easier, the right words will come to you when you need them, and you will indeed be a better person. That is the secret to spirituality, and it has nothing at all to do with believing in an immortal soul, or in anything supernatural.*[2] (Daniel Dennett. *Breaking the Spell*)

Spirituality Versus Religion

In fact Daniel Dennett has come up with a pretty good scheme for becoming a better person and all of his ideas find strong support in the Bible. Parallels to each of his aspects of spirituality can be found in Jesus' teaching. (Appendix 1) However, his definition is lacking in several respects.

Caring for other people is a serious omission from Dennett's analysis. Perhaps it can be inferred from what he has said and maybe if spirituality had been the primary topic of his book he would have expanded his definition to include a clear reference to altruistic behavior but its absence is noticeable and significant.

Also in order to support his conclusion that spirituality has nothing at all to do with believing in an immortal soul or in anything supernatural he has to ignore dimensions of spirituality that definitely do require belief in the supernatural, just about any kind of prayer, for example. Nonetheless, Daniel Dennett has succeeded in defining an important area of overlap in the experience of believers and non-believers and this is a valuable insight on which we can build.

Now, something can be true whether or not you believe it and for me spirituality and God are inextricably linked. Therefore, it is the potential for undercover work by the Spirit of God that I want to explore. If God can influence us at the unconscious level of our minds without violating our free will to bring about beneficial change in our personality and behavior then our conscious beliefs become less relevant to the process of character construction. Those beliefs are still important but their significance lies elsewhere, as we shall see. So in this opening chapter I will attempt to unpack what Jesus has to say to the unbeliever.

I have written in the margin of Dennett's book alongside his definition of spirituality the words "repentance" and "childlikeness" because his definition reminds me of both those key themes of Jesus' gospel: a fundamental change of mind and attitude, humbly moving the focus of interest away from self to the larger world of which we are just a small part, resulting in wiser speech and actions. You can do this, as Daniel Dennett says, without believing in anything beyond the material world. He has described one of the most important spiritual transitions a person can make: dying to self and self-attitudes. He has found words that can be equally meaningful and acceptable to people of all beliefs or none. Here is something we can agree upon despite our many and varied ideas about the nature or even the existence of God.

One can be selfless without being a believer. It is possible to have a humble mind without being a theist. One can be awestruck by the wonders of nature without seeing them as created by a Person. One can be focused and engaged with the moment and wise in speech and action without having faith in God. One can work at being a better person without the knowledge and encouragement of a heavenly Father.

God Incognito

The first key word from Jesus is "repentance". Repentance means changing one's mind. It is recognizing that one's thoughts words or actions have been wrong and taking steps to change them. You do not need to believe in God to do that. The writer to the Hebrews defines the deepest foundational layer of the spiritual life as "repentance from dead works". [3] That which is dead has ceased to make any contribution to life and can only putrefy and infect if left lying around but cutting out mental gangrene does not necessarily require a theistic belief system.

Then there is "childlikeness". On at least one occasion Jesus called a little child to him and setting him in the center of the listening crowd he told them that unless they were to be converted and become as little children they would by no means enter the kingdom of heaven. All three Synoptic Gospels report such an incident.[4]

Can a person "humble themselves as a little child" without believing in God? Daniel Dennett speaks of "an attitude of humble curiosity". Young children have an endless capacity for asking questions. You tell her something and she says "Why?" So you scratch your head and offer an explanation only to hear the question repeated. This goes on until she has whittled the subject down to something that fits into her experience. I believe God wants us to question in humility and not stop until we arrive at something solid enough to make sense. We should never believe anything that we are not prepared to think deeply about and that must include questioning and challenging the existence of God. Jesus is calling for a change in our thinking that results in us becoming spiritually like a little child. I do not believe that young children are perfect – we all know that is not true – but their minds have a certain freedom from bias and they are easily led, hence Jesus' dire warning to adults who corrupt young children.

When my daughter was about five or six we were in a clothes shop to buy her a dressing gown. My wife was trying to talk her into choosing a particular gown that she liked but my daughter was digging her heels in because she thought it looked too babyish. I was standing by watching them get more and more frustrated with each other until an idea occurred to me. I pointed out to my daughter that this gown in its general appearance looked rather like one already owned by her mother. That did the trick and we left the store with our purchase and everyone happy.

Jesus tells us we must return to a state of childlike mental freedom and allow ourselves to be led by God. Our Father is always capable of seeing the best way forward and we must respond in humility to the inner voice of conviction. The result will be the forgiveness of our waywardness and the discovery of a personal agenda that has at least some resemblance to the mind of God. In other words we will have entered God's kingdom. I think it is possible to hear and respond to that inner voice of conviction, conscience if you like, without necessarily recognizing it as God. The Holy Spirit can and does work incognito.

Dolphins and Dawkins

An atheist with a humble questioning attitude would say that they are not aware of evidence sufficient to convince them of the existence of God, and certainly there is no infallible proof of God's existence that I have come across. But then neither is there any such proof of God's non-existence. Philosophers have been arguing about it for centuries and more recently scientists have entered on both sides of the fray. Nobody can produce a knockout punch because it is impossible to prove or disprove the existence of someone who cannot be objectively detected inside our reality system. And if there were such a person who could be so detected then they would not be God; they would be just another part of the system. This does not mean, however, that reasons to believe in a personal benevolent creator cannot be sought and found.

For me the idea of God offers the best explanation for why there is anything at all, why space, time, matter and energy actually exist and how it is that I exist as an individual person possessing the freedom of mind to be able to ask that searching question, "Why is there anything at all?" In company with many and probably most other believers I did not come to my faith through intellectual investigation but through personal experience. Nevertheless, for me it will always be important to use every opportunity to check the reasonableness of what I believe to be true.

Borrowing some words from John Robinson's *Honest to God* I believe that what lies at the heart of things and governs their workings is personal.[5] At the beginning and the end, the top and the bottom and in or under or behind every individual part of physical reality but extending infinitely beyond it is the ground of my being, a person whom I call God. But what kind of God do I believe in?

By and large our ideas about God sit somewhere between two poles. At one extreme is Deism, the idea that God created and energized the universe but then so to speak stepped back, sat down and became a spectator. Deism does not work for me. I recall the thrill I experienced when dangling my fingers into the open top of a large tank at Sea World; I discovered that fish can enjoy and seek out human contact. In a similar vein I remember the gospel singer Barry McGuire telling the story of how he spent a hilarious hour as a teenager leaning over the side of a fishing boat off the Californian coast while a school of dolphins jostled for position to have him whack their noses with a knotted towel. We reach out to other creatures and they respond to us.

Animals also care about other animals not of their own kind like the pet dog refusing to leave the burning family home in order to protect four tiny kittens trapped inside.[6] If God is responsible for creating animals capable of that kind of behavior then I find it impossible to see him as a deistic zookeeper. However, Deism does emphasize an important aspect of God's nature.

Many great scientists have held a Deistic view of God and even Richard Dawkins admits to respecting people who hold this view today. The reason is that Deism sits comfortably with the self-governing nature of the universe that is embodied in the laws of physics. Our idea of God needs to recognize that he has created something that does not need him to constantly intervene from outside the system in order for the creation to function properly. God has built into the universe an enormous amount of potential for self-management and invention.

The Caring Creator

At the other extreme in our notions of divinity is Pantheism, the idea that God is in every particle of the universe but has no existence independent of the universe. Richard Dawkins refers to Pantheism as "sexed-up Atheism". It seems that some materialists can go as far as believing in a cosmic mind arising out of and bound up with the physical universe but not a Creator who exists independently of it and extends infinitely beyond it while causing and indwelling every part of it. When you boil it all down it is the idea of a personal God that Dawkins is objecting to and that is what you get when you join Pantheism to Deism: a Creator who cares.

The Bible presents us with a God who encompasses the two very different qualities of transcendence and immanence, the extremes of both holiness and intimacy. [7] He is the cause of but he is also involved in and, therefore, he cares deeply about his creation. Sometimes it helps me to think of God as the supreme scientist, the master engineer who has set up this universe with all of its amazing and endless self-regulating and creative complexity. At other times I can feel the Spirit of God closer to me than the air that I am breathing. Through the interplay of these very different channels of communication I come to understand and experience the Father-love of God the Creator of all things and I am drawn into a personal relationship with him.

To me this whole God package is intensely real but in a strictly scientific sense it is un-provable, a presupposition, an act of faith. However, there is only one other possibility that I can see, and that is atheism. This too is a presupposition, an act of faith. There are only two options; either somebody is causing physical reality or physical reality is just happening. The problem is that whenever I try to analyze these two alternative ideas, to assess and compare their reasonableness, I am quickly overwhelmed by the incomprehensibility of both concepts. I cannot really grasp either of them. Evidently I do not have the necessary mental equipment.

On the one hand an omnipotent personal Creator capable of achieving a predetermined end result while accommodating the uncertainties of human free will would need a mind large enough to respond to millions of human choices every second let alone all the other endless possibilities that are generated by the workings of chance in the universe. This pulverizes my imagination. It needs to be said, however, that this particular credibility gap is getting narrower as we develop ever more powerful super-computers.[8] The mind that endowed electrons and semiconductors with such huge potential for us to discover and use in this way must itself be even more immense than those machines.

On the other hand the idea that something just comes out of nothing seems totally ridiculous. If that process could ever be defined in a mathematically based "Theory of Everything" then where would that theory have come from? If it had been composed in our minds then it could hardly explain the existence of those minds; but if it had pre-existed us and we had merely discovered it then we would be back at the root problem without having explained anything. The mathematics would need either to have come spontaneously into existence out of nothing or to have been created.

Yet despite both these ideas being way beyond my grasp one of them must be correct. Therefore, you can choose to be a "Bright" who believes physical reality is just happening ex nihilo or, like me, you can choose to be a "Smart" who thinks a bet on God is a good investment. If God turns out to have been nothing more than an interesting but erroneous theory I will never know! If a Bright is mistaken then, if they have unwisely relied on belief in God's non-existence to justify a life of callousness or cruelty towards others, there could be one "hell" of a shock awaiting them.

In response to this paradox I think that Jesus proclaimed a message of forgiveness and entry to the kingdom that did not require belief in God. Did he realize that implication? I very much doubt it. Jesus would never have met a scientific humanist and probably not any other kind of atheist so he never had to deal with such ideas. Yet even if Jesus did not anticipate exactly how we might interpret his teaching in the twenty-first century he did understand the importance of meeting people where they were in their life with the minimum of preconditions. He has defined the entry qualification of the kingdom as a universal spiritual principle, repentant childlikeness. This door is open to all regardless of their beliefs.

Repentant Childlikeness

Of course, as people who have experienced the reality of God's indwelling presence we Christians will want to take the opportunity, when it arises, to encourage non-believers to seek after God but we must, like Jesus, engage with people where they are now. We have to be prepared to present the ideas of childlikeness and repentance from dead works as being the way for all of us to become better people and for the world to become a better place. So these days when I talk to my atheist and agnostic friends I try to avoid intellectual confrontation. We speak about how we should be living our lives and thereby discover much common ground to be explored. It is great if that leads on to sharing my experience of God but only if it is the right time and place to do so.

I used to think my job was to make sure that as many people as possible would hear and believe in the good news about Jesus Christ's death and resurrection because that was the only certain way we can be "saved" in the eschatological sense. By that I mean being excused for our actions when we eventually come to give account of our lives to God. I believe in that courtroom drama of the final judgment, as did Jesus. I also believe that it is only because of Jesus' obedience in being willing to die on the cross that vast numbers of humans will be made righteous. However, I now see that Jesus placed great emphasis on living better in this present life and saw this as the pathway to moral exoneration in the next. He taught that our destiny beyond this world depends on our actions rather than our beliefs, and the first action required of us is to repent.

Repentance is a major theme in the Synoptic Gospels. "Repent" was his first public pronouncement. Jesus said he had come to call sinners to repentance and he commissioned his disciples to go on preaching until repentance and remission of sins had been shared with all nations. They started out well on this task. The punch line of Peter's sermon on the day of Pentecost was, "Repent and be baptized in the name of Jesus Christ for the remission of sins". His second sermon in Solomon's Porch again majored on repentance, mentioning "faith" only in relation to the miraculous healing of a lame man. But after a while the message began to change. "Belief" or "faith" became increasingly prominent.[9]

By the time the fourth Gospel was written late in the first century it was possible for the author to give an account of Jesus' life and ministry without a single use of the word "repent". I'm not joking. Zilch! Clean sheet! Not one mention. John's Gospel is all about "believing". "Repentance" is off the radar screen, although in fairness to John he does record Jesus telling a couple of people to "go and sin no more". (See Appendix 2 for a detailed study on repentance versus belief in Jesus' teaching)

Honest Doubt

Does it matter if the message has changed? I think it does. Repentance is something that everybody should be able to understand and put into effect. Believing the truth of the resurrection of Jesus Christ, on the other hand, requires a quantum jump in the mind. No sensible person is going to accept as a fact that a man has risen from the dead without first thoroughly investigating the matter and carefully weighing the evidence. Even then on the basis of experience they may still reject the idea. In fact there are many professing Christians who believe in a spiritual but not a literal physical resurrection. Thomas, one of the twelve disciples, would not believe it until he was confronted with the risen Jesus and Matthew, with disarming candor, reports that "some doubted" even when they were so confronted.[10] (He was actually referring to the eleven disciples – twelve minus Judas Iscariot – so they must have later come to believe because all of them were present and active on the Day of Pentecost, but only after having doubted.)

Would God place such an intellectual hurdle in the way of forgiveness? Significantly in Luke's account of the Great Commission the message that the risen Jesus gave to the disciples to preach in his name was encapsulated in the phrase "repentance and the remission of sins". [11] Even at this late stage, with the living proof of the resurrection before their eyes in the very person of Jesus back from the dead, he did not lay down belief in his resurrection as a necessary condition of forgiveness; only repentance was required.

Given the unavailability of an infallible proof for the existence of God and the skepticism of some of the original witnesses to the Resurrection a belief-based final judgment on how we have lived our lives when we stand before God seems morally unfair. However, even if it were ethically well grounded it could still only be logically justified if there were many more people who have had access to the story of Jesus Christ than who have not. But that is far from being the case; knowledge is the exception, ignorance the rule. Living as we do in a world where Christianity is the largest religion and communications are global we could easily assume that virtually all of the seven plus billion people alive today have heard of Jesus. This is not so but even if it were it would still only be a very small part of the story because we need to take account of all the humans who have ever existed, not just those who are still around in the twenty-first century.

The results of four different academic studies indicate that between 50 and 100 billion humans have lived on earth since the beginning of time.[12] First, there were all the people who lived and died in the thousands of years before Jesus was born. (Perhaps 100,000 years if you accept the majority scientific view.) Then for the first 1500 years after Christ he was virtually unknown outside Europe and parts of the Orient and Africa. It is only in the last 500 years, since Europeans started to explore and colonize Africa, Asia, Australia and the Americas, that many people in those areas would have even had a chance to hear his name and it is only in the last half century or so that the spread of radio and literacy would have made knowledge of Jesus Christ possible other than by word of mouth. It seems certainly the case that many billions of people have lived and died without knowledge of Christ.

How could a God of justice and love prioritise moral exoneration to a tiny minority of humans who possess knowledge only obtainable from the Bible and who have been fortunate enough to have lived in an era that accounts for less than one percent of the entire period of humanity's existence? Thankfully, according to the gospel of the kingdom that Jesus preached, it is not the knowledge or lack of knowledge of any particular set of truths that matters. What matters is repentant childlikeness. Knowing about Jesus Christ, believing in his resurrection, even believing in God is not what gains us entry to the kingdom of heaven. The importance of belief in those truths emerges at a later stage on the road we will be traveling in this book; at the gate of the kingdom they are unnecessary.

Finding Better Options

Jesus' gospel of the kingdom can be transposed as follows. Repent, change your inner person by changing your thinking, and become as a little child. Make any necessary reparation. If you do this then the guilt and shame concerning your past behavior that burdens your present and blights your future will be lifted from you. You will be set free from the bondage of your history and your anxieties. Shift the focus of your attention from your own concerns to the needs of the other person and you will become wiser in your speech and actions. Whether you realize it or not you will have taken the vital step across the threshold of eternal life and if you persist in that disposition of repentant childlikeness day-by-day and hour-by-hour you will continue as a subject in God's kingdom. Your life will come under the moral government of God, whether you believe in him or not.

People in all times and places with whatever personal or collective beliefs they held about the nature of reality could and did discover this spiritual principle. They have found that good things flow from having the mind, the inner person, focus its attention on something other than its own self-centered interests and desires. They have found fresh creativity and liberty by purging their thinking, words and actions of that which seeks to enslave or exploit other people.

In the coming chapters we will see that God's plan is to get everyone into the kingdom but not necessarily to get everyone into the church. When all are in the kingdom there will no longer be any need for a key holder. The church is a temporary phenomenon, a means to an end. When the job is completed the church will be no more.[13] Our objective as Christians is to be the catalyst for establishing the kingdom and in so doing we will eventually work ourselves out of a job. When the lump is completely leavened the yeast has no further purpose.

Our primary task as Christians is neither persuasion nor preaching; it is prayer. We have a vast power at our disposal to sway the course of events and to change the thinking and behavior of people without them knowing anything about it. Our priority must be to discover how we can effectively carry out our real job in the world, bringing about change in a way that faithfully preserves people's freedom of choice while intervening through the spiritual realm to enable them to find and choose better options. This is God's way. We are to be the house of prayer for all nations. We are here to open people's eyes to the merits of the dressing gown they have been ignoring or rejecting because they considered it too childish.

In this work the church is to collaborate with the Great Intercessor, Jesus, who ever lives to make intercession for us and all those others who will come to God through him. During his time on earth he showed us what could be achieved through a total commitment to seeking the face of God in prayer. His teachings are full of encouragement and guidance on this vital subject. The kingdom of heaven is to be actualized on the earth through the prayers of the saints.

Skeptical Sympathizers

We serve the King whenever we respond to the needs of a fellow human. Conversely, when we fail to attend to those needs we are overlooking or ignoring Jesus. In effect we will meet Jesus many times in our life without realizing it. We do not need to have read the Bible or belong to a church or even be aware of the existence of either the Bible or the church. We may or may not be following some religious path. We may not even believe in God. Yet we will happen upon Jesus whenever we meet another human in need and our response to that person is our response to him.[14]

By adopting a humble, inquiring and teachable daily walk with God, if we believe in God, but if not then in a focused and engaged relationship with our fellow humans, conscious of and concerned for their needs and problems and aspirations, willing to put ourselves out in order to serve them, we dispose ourselves to the kind of righteous behavior that gains us entry to the kingdom. This counts for more than religious practices.[15]

Of course, Christians know that God gets no pleasure from human unbelief and to serve the Lord effectively we must believe in him.[16] Progress as a disciple of Jesus depends upon our trust in God and I do not think that an atheistic spirituality will ever be able to tap into the creative and healing power that offers us the only real opportunity to defeat evil in this world. This book will investigate how believers can become more effective servants of the king and play their part in establishing the kingdom of God. I hope you will stay with me as I seek to explore this theme through to its grand finale. However, when it comes to getting right with God on a personal level, taking the first step into the spiritual life, I think our Father is looking for the death of our self-centeredness. Such will allow his entry through the back door of the spirit rather than the front door of the mind.

If Richard Dawkins and Daniel Dennett genuinely cannot see any reason to believe in a personal creator at the core of reality then will God on those grounds censure or reject them? I imagine I can hear that One on the throne as it might be when we come before him to give account of our stewardship:

"So Richard, you didn't believe in me. Got enough evidence now? Anyway, never mind all that God delusion stuff. Let's talk about those sick people and what you did for them."

"Now you, Daniel, I seem to recall saying, "For goodness sake let's try to get food and clothing to everybody who needs them as soon as possible." Well then, did you?"

"And you, Roger, when exactly did you visit me in prison?"

There was silence in heaven for about half an hour.

Chapter 2

Mary's Story

The large man shouldering a hefty wooden beam filled most of the narrow street and he stopped to let Mary squeeze past with a radiant smile. A fleeting expression of sadness passed across his face, as he seemed to find the answer to an unspoken question but then the intense warmth returned. Mary would find it difficult to forget that smile.

Then a couple of days later she saw the joiner again in the wealthy district where most of her clients lived. A new house was being built and he was on the roof absorbed in his work but he spotted her. She returned his cheery wave feeling as if she had known him all her life.

Some time later when the charismatic builder with the large smile had become better known for other reasons Mary got word he was due to dine with one of her clients. Not knowing quite why, but confident from her previous visits that the doorkeeper would let her in, she headed for the house. Mingling with other women by the dining room door she listened to the builder telling stories about birds and seeds, fishes and nets. He talked with passion about a caring heavenly Father who desired to forgive and befriend his human children. Mary felt overwhelmed by a deep longing to know this builder's God.

Then suddenly it became clear why she had come to Simon's house. With her heart pounding she stepped into the room and stood at the end of the couch on which he was reclining. Sobbing uncontrollably she knelt down and a flood of tears soaked his feet. She loosened her glorious waist length hair, using it as a towel. On a cord around her neck was a flask of fragrant oil. She kissed his feet, anointed them with the oil and gently massaged the calloused skin.

She felt the unspoken thoughts of astonishment, disapproval and dismay coming from Simon. The builder must have felt them too because he told Simon a story about a couple of people who were in debt. Then he turned to her with that beaming smile, this time without a trace of sadness, and said, "Your sins are forgiven; your faith has saved you; go in peace." She fled the house feeling embarrassed but clean and reborn.

* * *

The afternoon was hot and dusty and Mary was glad it was her turn to ride one of the few donkeys they had with them. Walking alongside was her new friend Magdalene whom she had recognized among the women listening to the builder in Simon the Pharisee's house. Most people knew Magdalene. She was the town's wild child, unpredictable and scary, but she had looked different on the day of the anointing, composed and relaxed. The knowing smile and caring touch on Mary's arm as she left in haste had encouraged Mary to seek her out the very next day. Magdalene had quite a story of her own to tell. Jesus, the builder, had prayed for her and from that moment good changes had started to happen in her life. Magdalene was a big fan of Jesus.

Mary had poured out her heart to Magdalene. She spoke about her unhappiness as a teenager in Bethany after her parents had died and how she just could not get along with her older sister, Martha, who had taken over running the household and family. One day she had left home vowing never to return. Joining a caravan headed north had certainly distanced her from her problems but she had paid a costly fare for the journey; the rich trader had taken her under his wing – and into his bed.

He had, however, treated her with kindness, leaving her in Galilee with money and a flask of rare perfume. He told her that this spikenard oil had come from a country of high mountains many months' journey to the east and if she ever found herself short of cash it would fetch enough to meet her needs for a whole year. Fortunately her looks and brains had allowed her to choose her customers carefully and she had prospered, but money could never wipe out the shame and unhappiness that always nagged at the back of her mind.

It was Magdalene who had come up with the way for her to leave

Galilee and her life of prostitution and return home to Bethany. Jesus was planning a visit to Jerusalem with twelve of his closest men and several wealthy women who regularly gave up their domestic comforts to support this group who would be traveling with him. Mary could join them.

So here she was on the road south getting to know these fascinating people. Simon Peter, built like the rock that was his nickname, a fisherman, impulsive but generous and kind; James and John, brothers and also fishermen, explosively intense but deeply compassionate; Matthew, formerly a tax collector; Joanna, whose husband Chuza worked for the king; these and the others, all of them devoted to the joiner-builder, Jesus, from Nazareth.

Jesus was amazing, only thirty something but with a depth of wisdom that made it seem as if he had been around for centuries. Whenever he talked to Mary it felt as if she was the most important person in the world. He had calmed her fears about returning to Bethany and she had seen him in action enough times to know that he could be trusted to handle any situation. Some of the stuff that happened around him defied logical explanation; Simon told her that Jesus had recently stopped a life-threatening storm. On that evidence Martha would be unlikely to present him with much of a problem.

* * *

Their arrival in Bethany had been sensational. At the outskirts of the village Jesus had called the party to a halt while he and Mary went on to her old home. Martha had been in the garden when they arrived. Whatever her first words might have been at this unexpected reappearance of the prodigal sister who had stormed out of the house five years before, they remained unsaid. Jesus had quietly taken command of the moment and in no time at all Mary found herself wrapped in Martha's arms. Then Lazarus had come from the house to join the emotional reunion. Mary had gaped in astonishment at her kid brother who now stood head and shoulders above her and looked like he would soon be matching Jesus in stature.

Martha, as always hospitable, had insisted on accommodating the entire party. Although the family home was large they needed help from neighbors to find everyone a bed. In the morning the travelers had moved on but here they were again on their next trip to the south.

Mary, eager to catch up with all that had been happening in Galilee, was completely absorbed in the stories Jesus was telling. Martha, however, was stressed out. The usually well-oiled domestic machine was sputtering and faltering at the very time when it needed to run smoothly. She appealed to Jesus to remind Mary of her responsibilities but he told her not to worry, everything would be fine. Martha calmed down and joined the group around him in the lounge. Mary looked at her sister and noticed a change; Jesus' wisdom had started to work.

* * *

Supper was being served in Bethany. Jesus was there, now on his fourth visit. Lazarus was reclining close to Jesus at the table, hanging on his every word. That Lazarus was even present at all was amazing because on Jesus' previous visit Lazarus had been dead. Yes, dead!

For weeks Martha and Mary had nursed their brother but his health had steadily declined despite all the attention of the doctors. Fearing the worst they had sent messengers to look for Jesus. So many sick people had responded to Jesus' prayers that he must surely be able to help, but there was no reply. Finally came the day they had been dreading when Lazarus' lifeless body was laid to rest in the cave that was their family tomb.

Then four days' later Jesus had arrived. Martha had heard the news first and gone out to meet him. Martha was a different woman these days; she had been discovering faith. "Even now", she had said to Jesus, "I know that whatever you ask of God he will give you." Jesus had come to the tomb and ordered the stone that covered the mouth of the cave to be removed. "I am the resurrection and the life," he had said to the onlookers. Then he had called out to Lazarus – and the young man had walked out of the cave.

Not everyone who had witnessed that miracle was pleased and there had been rumors of a plot to kill Jesus being hatched up by certain authorities who saw him as a threat to their own position. He had immediately gone away to Ephraim but here he was again, two miles from Jerusalem and in deadly danger. Mary sensed that this might be the last time she would see Jesus alive and her final chance to thank him for all he had done for her.

The jar of costly spikenard perfume, that symbolic reminder of the life she had lived and left behind, was still in her room. She fetched it, and with the memory of that other occasion vividly replaying in her mind she came up behind Jesus, anointing his feet and wiping them with her hair. There was lotion enough to pour it liberally over his head as well as his feet and the rich fragrance filled every part of the house. Jesus, knowing what was in Mary's mind, told the guests that she had been keeping this for the day of his burial and that what she had done would be told all over the world wherever the gospel was preached. She knew then that her intuition had been right. She inhaled the glorious aroma and relived that amazing sense of forgiveness she had felt in Simon the Pharisee's house.

* * *

$1400 per Ounce!

In the previous chapter I welcomed Daniel Dennett's analysis of spirituality because it helps to establish common ground between believers and unbelievers. Given that the existence of the supernatural cannot be proved or disproved there is nothing to be gained, other than the pleasure of scoring points in a debate, by disputation. The problems facing humanity require urgent attention and we cannot afford to waste our time and energy on beating each other up. Jesus' gospel embraces this sentiment. If you are an unbeliever then perhaps you can at least explore the ideas of childlikeness and repentance and become a skeptical sympathizer, living by the inner voice of conscience and allowing space for those of us who see a different reality. We will do our best to reciprocate.

Useful though Dennett's scheme of spirituality is, however, it falls short in several important respects. I have already pointed out that it leaves no room for prayer, something that all Christians would regard as important, and it makes no specific mention of concern for the welfare of other people. That leads us to its most glaring omission; love. This most intense human emotion, this most powerful human experience, this most valued human quality apparently finds no place in Dennett's scheme of spirituality. By contrast love is at the heart of Jesus' gospel and nowhere is this clearer than in the story of a redeemed prostitute that Jesus predicted would be told all over the world.

Now I need to make a confession about Mary's story. All four gospels contain an account of a woman anointing Jesus with perfume. The stories are similar enough that if you had only read through the Gospels once or twice you would probably remember them as four slightly different versions of the same tale. However, I have read the relevant passages enough times to know that actually there are two different stories. Yet I have retold them as if they were linked, two parts of the same woman's life. I have combined Luke's story of a Galilean prostitute with John's account of the saintly Mary of Bethany and I have done this because I believe the two stories belong together.[1]

I didn't always think that. Modern day Protestant scholars are generally of the view that there are two quite distinct stories – one about an unnamed prostitute who lived in Galilee in the north of Israel and another about a different woman who lived in Bethany near Jerusalem in the south of the country whose name was Mary – and for many years I was happy to go along with that angle. However, after chatting with my local guru in biblical studies I became aware that many Roman Catholic scholars, particularly those from earlier centuries, have been of the opinion that actually it was one joined-up story. So I came to think that perhaps the matter was not cut and dried. My mind was opened to fresh thinking.

Then one day I was pondering the story in John's Gospel chapter twelve about a woman, called Mary, who went and fetched a sealed flask of rare perfume, broke it open, emptied it over Jesus' feet and wiped them with her hair. Onlookers said the perfume was worth more than 300 denarii and objected to the waste of something so precious. One denarius was a laborer's daily pay, an amount equivalent to the United Kingdom National Minimum Wage of around £50 ($75) at the time of writing. So this perfume was worth about £15000 ($22500) in the money value of the early twenty-first century. If you factor in John's statement that there was one pound of ointment in the flask then this stuff was worth $1400 per ounce. Search the Internet for the world's most expensive perfumes and you will find that spikenard oil, if still available at that same price, would be around number five. This story was starting to grab my attention.

What If?

How did Mary come by sixteen ounces of the most expensive perfume in the world, extracted from a Nepalese plant some 3000 miles from her home? What was the back-story to this extraordinary anointing? It is, or at least it used to be, men who give expensive perfume as presents to women but if Mary was married then why is there no mention of a husband by either Luke or John who both knew the details of Mary's family situation? These Bethany folk were comfortably off (it seems they owned a private tomb) but that does not come close to explaining the perfume. Today it would only be billionaire oil tycoons and the like who could afford such extravagance.

And how was it that Jesus appeared to know about the perfume and Mary's intended use for it? It seems they must have discussed it at some time prior to the anointing at Bethany. Why would they need to have talked about a flask of perfume?

Then came the what-if question. What if the saintly Mary of Bethany and the unnamed Galilean prostitute had been one and the same? If this link were real it would answer both the above questions. It would provide an explanation for how Mary came by a flask of extremely valuable perfume without having a man in her life. [2] It would also explain why Mary might have raised the subject of the perfume with Jesus since the earnings of prostitution are condemned in both the Law of Moses and the prophetic writings. What a delightfully creative solution from Jesus to the problem of how to get rid of such an embarrassing possession. [3]

Furthermore, this connecting of the two stories had the ability to make sense of several other things in the Gospels. For example, Jesus often referred to tax collectors as being typical of those outcasts of society who were becoming his followers and we know that Matthew, one of his disciples, had been a tax collector. [4] But on at least one occasion he mentioned prostitutes and tax collectors in the same breath as examples of people who were coming into the kingdom of God. [5] If there were also a former prostitute among his disciples then that would stack up: Jesus would have been referring to Mary and Matthew.

And again it would make sense of two very unusual coincidences about the two stories. In each case the woman anointed Jesus' feet (when it would have been normal to anoint the head) and in each case she wiped them with her hair. Why would she have wiped perfume off Jesus' feet with her hair? Tears, yes, but why perfume? If two different women, at opposite ends of the country were involved without TV, radio, Twitter or even a newspaper to convey such specific details the double coincidence is remarkable. If, on the other hand, it was Mary on both occasions then her impulse to re-enact the event that had changed her life, while investing it with the deeper significance of anticipating Jesus' death, is understandable.[6]

Wholehearted Sacrificial Devotion

However, what hit me the hardest was the way in which the joined-up story would explain the extraordinary devotion of Mary. If Jesus had been the one who rescued her from a life of prostitution then we can totally understand why she loved him the way she did. And we can also see why Jesus would have selected her story to accompany the preaching of his gospel throughout the entire world. Suddenly I was beginning to feel the intensity of spikenard love.

To understand what I mean by spikenard love you will need to think about Mary's family. Martha seems to have been the dominant character in the household, which suggests that she was single, her parents were no longer living and that Lazarus was her junior by quite some years. Martha was a practical person who always wanted to do her best as a hostess. The big thing we know about Lazarus is that Jesus raised him from the dead but there is little else recorded about him suggesting he was the youngest of the three siblings. Mary seems to have been the middle in age and it is not difficult to imagine her as a strong minded teenager, depressed by the deaths of her father and mother, clashing with her older sister Martha's controlling tendencies and running away from home. Luke and John give us enough details about this family for us to see a pattern in their story.

Martha was a hardworking, caring kind of person who discovered from being around Jesus how to channel her gifts in the right direction and modify her expectations of those who did not share her task-oriented focus. She learned how to serve with love and out of that love came a strong faith in Jesus' ability to save and heal.

Lazarus' love for Jesus was forever secured by his miraculous return from the dead. How could he ever fully express his gratitude to the Lord for what he had done for him? In the final scene of the story at Bethany, Lazarus is found sitting at the supper table soaking up everything Jesus has to say.

Mary was a worshipper. She sensed something that others missed. She was in tune with Jesus. The road to Calvary was weighing heavily on her mind, and she had to give tangible expression to her devotion to the Lord. The anointing with costly spikenard represented Mary's willingness to sacrifice all that she was and all that she possessed for the One who had healed her and assured her of forgiveness.

Martha's faithful service, Lazarus' grateful friendship and Mary's selfless adoration have valuable lessons to teach us about three important dimensions of love. When I first noticed this I shared the idea with my home church congregation one Sunday morning. Picking out words from John's account I tagged the three points of my message as Serving Love (Martha), Supping Love (Lazarus) and Spikenard Love (Mary). My listeners that day were, as I had been, moved and challenged by these thoughts. They murmured approval as I spoke about the practical service of Martha and they said "Amen" when I got to the warm friendship of Lazarus. But when I reached the priceless wholehearted sacrificial devotion of Mary you could have heard a pin drop. They asked me to preach the next Sunday and talk some more about spikenard love. I think that is the only time I have ever had an encore in church.

If the woman of Luke chapter seven and Mary of Bethany were one and the same, then we have a beautiful explanation of the depth of her love for Jesus resulting from the way in which he had rescued her. Jesus said that the story of Mary's anointing would be told wherever the gospel was preached all over the world, implying that it was unique. Yet uniqueness is really only possible if Mary had been responsible for both anointings. If that is the case then Jesus would have been emphasizing her whole story, and it is the whole story that brilliantly illustrates the power of Jesus' gospel.

On numerous occasions after connecting the two parts of the story I returned to it, but a few more years went by before I realized where it was taking me. In saying that this story would be told wherever the gospel was preached anywhere in the world Jesus was implying that Mary's story had particular relevance to the gospel message. At that point I found myself starting to ask questions about the nature of Jesus' gospel.

Good News about What?

Although I had been reading and studying the Bible for more than fifty years in all that time I had never really taken on board the emphasis in Jesus' words. Of course I knew the stories of the anointings and I was aware of what Jesus had said about the Bethany anointing becoming well known but I had always thought that since this story is recorded in the Bible and since the Bible is internationally distributed the story is out there in the public domain. But then I was struck by what Jesus actually said:

> *Wherever this gospel is preached in the whole world, what this woman has done will also be told.*[7]

I realized that the words "preach" and "tell" imply active communication and not just passive publication. Jesus was at the very least expecting, and was arguably prescribing, that Mary's story should become a vital part of the message of his gospel. Yet in all my years as a lay preacher I had told the story only once, that day when I spoke in church about serving love, supping love and spikenard love. Moreover, I could not recall ever having heard anyone else tell it in public. This minor revelation was proving to be the thin end of an awkward wedge. If I had been overlooking for so long such an important fact then what else had I been missing? What else did Jesus say was to be included in his message? What is the good news that Jesus himself brought and taught? In short, what exactly is the gospel of Jesus Christ?

As I started to dig into these questions I came to see that the reason why they had not come up previously was because of my belief in the Resurrection and the divinity of Christ. The story of Jesus has come to be primarily about his death on the cross and his subsequent rising from the grave. All four Gospels cover in depth those important events that occurred in a certain Passover week about two thousand years ago and they dominate the rest of the New Testament. It was inevitable that a man rising from the dead should become the focus of attention for Christians, the central part of our belief system and I am sure that it will continue to be the case for me for the rest of my life. However, there is another side to the matter: the good news delivered by Jesus. This relates to the message that he communicated, the actual words that came out of his mouth and the healings and miracles that demonstrated and reinforced the truth of his teaching.

Now if Jesus had lived an exemplary life, died on the cross and been raised from the dead, but had said very little, then the gospel of Jesus Christ would necessarily have to be about the events of his life rather than his words. It would be the good news about Jesus Christ. Without any record of his teaching we would have been obliged to focus solely on his life story, his death, his resurrection and his ascension as seen by others. However, that is not the case. He said an enormous amount about many different subjects and he made it very clear that he had come to proclaim the gospel.

Rediscovering Jesus

During the three years in which Jesus conducted his public ministry and trained the twelve apostles he was delivering his gospel in words and actions. As I started to look into this I became increasingly aware that I had been guilty of giving insufficient attention to Jesus and focusing instead on what other people had said about Jesus, even people who wrote parts of the Bible. Paul, for example, tells us a lot of good news about Jesus but tells us hardly anything spoken by Jesus; in fact he quotes Jesus on only two occasions. [8] (Sorry, Paul; you're still my hero!)

The gospel Paul preached is that our salvation depends upon receiving and holding onto three pieces of information about Jesus:

- Christ died for our sins
- He was buried
- He rose again the third day[9]

Now I hold these facts to be crucial in God's plan for the human race and they have deep meaning for me. They mark Jesus out as totally unique, they provide me with the basis and direction for my life in this age, and they underpin my hope of experiencing eternal life. However, this message cannot be the gospel that Jesus brought because Jesus' gospel was being preached before any of these things happened. The gospel Jesus taught is contained in his words, spoken during his lifetime and nearly all of those words were spoken prior to the cross. When Jesus said that his gospel of the kingdom would be preached all over the world he was still a wandering Galilean prophet, not the one who had been declared to be the Son of God with power by the resurrection from the dead.

Forgive me if I seem to be laboring this point but I imagine that many Christians will think, as I used to, that the gospel Jesus commissioned us to deliver throughout the entire world starts with the cross and the Resurrection. But that cannot be the case. Those events are vitally important but they are the climax not the corpus of Jesus' gospel, the punchline of the story but not the buildup. To get the whole picture we need to focus first on what Jesus actually said. Then, when we have thoroughly digested what he considered to be his gospel we need to integrate that message with the story of the cross, the Resurrection and the ascension.

I do not think that this is a once-for-all-time exercise, a neat theological repackaging process. If it were that easy I would not have been shying away from it for as long as I have. The more I understand of God and his ways the more I realize that we cannot build doctrinal gazebos for him to live in. The mercies of God are new every morning. Every day there is some fresh facet of his steadfast love to be revealed and enjoyed. All we can hope to do is get the basic rules of the game clearer in our minds. What happens when the players get onto the pitch is anybody's guess.

Truth Comes Alive

This is a huge subject and my objective is simply to awaken the reader's interest in revisiting the Gospels with an open mind. My starting point is the discovery that Jesus has highlighted Mary's story as an essential accessory to the proclamation of his gospel but where should we go from here? I find it significant that Mary's is the only biography that Jesus has specifically selected to go with the preaching of his gospel. There are many amazing stories in the Gospels but this is the only one that Jesus said would be told all over the world. So it was hardly surprising that when I started to study Mary's story I found that it features all the essential elements of Jesus' gospel. In this story we find, either in Jesus' actual words or implied by the events of the story, eight key components of his gospel:

- love
- sin
- forgiveness
- faith
- salvation
- peace
- repentance

- healing

All of these are vital parts of Jesus' message. So it seems fitting, indeed compelling, that we should adopt Mary's story as a map for our journey to rediscover the gospel of Jesus, the tale of a redeemed prostitute that Jesus said would be proclaimed worldwide. In the chapters that follow we will examine the truths represented by these words, seeking to understand what they mean and how they relate to and interact with each other.

As I developed this study I found myself remembering parts of my own story and some of these have ended up in the book. There is nothing about my life that is remarkable and little that is worthy of imitation and I appreciate that in being autobiographical I am taking the risk of boring my readers to death. I could have avoided this by drawing on the experiences of others, whose lives have been much more exciting than mine, to illustrate Jesus' gospel in action. However, mine is the only personal story to which I have direct firsthand access. As such it gives me inside knowledge and enables me to compare the experiences of people who lived two thousand years ago with what has happened to someone living in modern times. In following this plan perhaps I will be able to show how the gospel of Jesus becomes truly meaningful when we encounter it for ourselves, when the truth that is embedded in the pages of the Bible comes alive for us personally.

This book is about rediscovering Jesus and, of course, one can only rediscover what one has previously discovered. So I need to tell you a little bit about how it all began for me. That will be the starting point of the next chapter.

Chapter 3

Spikenard Love

Sometime early in 1951 at the age of eight I experienced my first serious God Moment. The emotions I underwent and the inner commitment I made at that time will be imprinted on my memory forever. I believe John Wesley was talking about a similar experience when he said that he "felt his heart strangely warmed" and I am happy to borrow his words to describe my own transition into the spiritual life. It came with an enigmatic cocktail of feelings – shame, forgiveness, acceptance and affirmation – mingled with an intense awareness of, but paradoxically a deep longing for, someone infinitely beyond myself who was capable of inspiring me to strive for and reach my full potential. I felt bathed in love, totally forgiven and completely at peace. I decided there and then that my life would be founded on a quest to know this person.

Of course I would not at the time have been able to describe the experience with the adult vocabulary I have just used. I would have said I had asked Jesus into my heart and actually that is still a perfectly good account of what happened. Whichever way I choose to talk about it this was the beginning of my personal journey towards God. I imagine that Mary experienced something similar when she came to Jesus in the house of Simon the Pharisee – she was having an intense God Moment – and the common denominator between her story and mine is a love relationship with Jesus.

> *Then one of the Pharisees asked him to eat with him. And he went to the Pharisee's house, and sat down to eat.*
>
> *And behold, a woman in the city who was a sinner, when she knew that Jesus sat at the table in the Pharisee's house, brought an*

alabaster flask of fragrant oil, and stood at his feet behind him weeping; and she began to wash his feet with her tears, and wiped them with the hair of her head; and she kissed his feet and anointed them with the fragrant oil.

Now when the Pharisee who had invited him saw this, he spoke to himself, saying, "This man, if he were a prophet, would know who and what manner of woman this is who is touching him, for she is a sinner."

And Jesus answered and said to him, "Simon, I have something to say to you." And he said, "Teacher, say it." "There was a certain creditor who had two debtors. One owed five hundred denarii, and the other fifty. And when they had nothing with which to repay, he freely forgave them both. Tell me, therefore, which of them will love him more?"

Simon answered and said, "I suppose the one to whom he forgave more." And he said to him, "You have rightly judged."

Then he turned to the woman and said to Simon, "Do you see this woman? I entered your house; you gave me no water for my feet, but she has washed my feet with her tears and wiped them with the hair of her head. You gave me no kiss, but this woman has not ceased to kiss my feet since the time I came in. You did not anoint my head with oil, but this woman has anointed my feet with fragrant oil. Therefore I say to you, her sins, which are many, are forgiven, for she loved much. But to whom little is forgiven, the same loves little."

And he said to her, "Your sins are forgiven."

And those who sat at the table with him began to say to themselves, "Who is this who even forgives sins?"

Then he said to the woman, "Your faith has saved you. Go in peace."[1]

Better Than Sex

The ease with which Mary gained access to Simon the Pharisee's house suggests she had been there before and knew Simon as a client. Luke says that it was when she heard that Jesus was dining with Simon that she decided on her course of action. What better way could there be to renounce prostitution and signal a change in her life than to do it in Simon's house? And from one who had known many "lovers" but without real love comes this moving act of love. Perhaps I am an incurable romantic but I find it impossible to read this story without being touched by the personal chemistry between Jesus and Mary, a man who apparently chose never to have a sexual relationship and a woman who probably wanted never to have another for the rest of her life.

I recall listening to an interview with Billy Graham some years ago in which he drew attention to Jesus' statement that humans in heaven will be like the angels in that they will neither give nor be given in marriage. He went on to remark, no doubt as the father of five children with a twinkle in his eye, that since Jesus seemed to be implying there would be no sexual intercourse in heaven then it could only be because there would be something even better to take its place!

I find it interesting that Jesus did not say there would be no gender in heaven. Personally I cannot imagine being anything other than masculine. Apart from those folk who find themselves inside a body of different gender to their psyche I guess this is true of most of us although several women have told me that if there is such a thing as reincarnation then they will be coming back as a man because men have such an easy life! My wife reminds me that when I was once asked a question about reincarnation in a quiz game at a party I said, applying similar logic, that I would like to come back as my cat. (Just joking, Lord!)

God willing in a few years' time I will celebrate half a century of marriage to Jose, the only woman I have ever known, in the biblical sense of that word. Yet I have also been blessed along the way with other close female friendships that have added important and valuable experiences to my life. In fact I would say that most of my closest friends have been women. Male friendships have been great, opening up dimensions of fellowship that can only be found in all-male company and I have loved men in a man's kind of way. Yet when it comes down to the most sensitive and meaningful things about life the male-female dynamic has always had some special quality.

The more I reflect on this it seems to me that the masculine-feminine thing is built into the cosmos at a fundamental level. It was C S Lewis who first suggested this to me when his space-traveling hero, Elwin Ransom, meets the governing archangels of the planets Mars and Venus:

Both the bodies were naked, and both were free from any sexual characteristics, either primary or secondary. That, one would have expected. But whence came this curious difference between them? He found he could point to no single feature wherein the difference resided, yet it was impossible to ignore. One could try – Ransom has tried a hundred times – to put it into words. He has said that Malacandra (Mars) was like rhythm and Perelandra (Venus) like melody. He has said that Malacandra affected him like a quantitative, Perelandra like an accentual, meter. He thinks that the first held in his hand something like a spear, but the hands of the other were open with the palms towards him. But I don't know that any of these attempts has helped me much. At all events what Ransom saw that moment was the real meaning of gender.

Gender is a reality, and a more fundamental reality than sex. Sex is, in fact, merely the adaptation to organic life of a fundamental polarity that divides all created beings. Female sex is simply one of the things that have feminine gender; there are many others, and masculine and feminine meet us on planes of reality where male and female would be simply meaningless. Masculine is not attenuated male, nor feminine attenuated female. On the contrary, the male and female of organic creatures are rather faint and blurred reflections of masculine and feminine.[2] (C S Lewis. *The Cosmic Trilogy*)

Adam and Eve

At the very beginning of the Bible we are told that God created humanity in his own image when he made them male and female. Then in the following chapters this idea is explored in the story of the first man and woman. Just let your imagination loose for a few moments and take a walk in the Garden of Eden.

Adam was quite smitten with Eve, to put it mildly! He had known there was something not quite right. God had brought all the animals to him, one by one, for Adam to give them names. They were a friendly bunch and he had a lot of fun with them but when sunset came they all went off in pairs to their nests and caves and he was left feeling lonely. One night he slept particularly heavily. It turned out subsequently that God had anaesthetized him to perform a surgical procedure that would solve his problem. (No, not Origen's operation!) When he woke up in the morning he wasn't alone; next to him was this exquisite creature, fast asleep. He just lay there spellbound, head propped on his elbow, eyes drinking in the view until it awoke.

That with a bit of elaboration on my part is how the Bible describes the start of the human journey. Creation followed by separation is the theme set by the first few verses of Genesis. So when, after creating everything else in the universe, God comes to humanity, the crown of his creation, then that is the way he does it; creation followed by separation. God didn't just remove a rib from Adam; he took half of Adam's personality. (If you are a woman you will probably be thinking that God took rather more than half and if you are a man you will probably be grateful that he did!) The image of God is portrayed by the two halves of the human race functioning in their proper relationship to each other and that relationship at its best is the strongest and deepest and fullest love that exists anywhere inside the cosmos.

It appears that this masculine-feminine polarity is a fundamental aspect of the nature of the Creator and it has been embossed onto every part of the creation. The deepest reality upon which the universe rests is love, a joyful, creative tension energized by the attraction between two opposites neither of which is complete without the other. (See Appendix 3)

It seems this principle will be carried over into the eternal destiny of the human race. The apostle Paul sees marriage as a picture of the relationship between Christ and his church [3] and John writes at the end of the Book of Revelation:

> *I saw a new heaven and a new earth, for the first earth had passed away. Also there was no more sea. Then I, John, saw the holy city, new Jerusalem, coming down from God, prepared as a bride adorned for her husband.*[4]

So it seems we are back with Billy Graham's "something better than sex" and perhaps in Mary's story we are getting a faint impression of what that something might actually look like. And that would give us a very good reason why Jesus picked her story out as the primary example of his gospel at work. With that in mind let us return to the script.

Love Covers All Sins

When Simon the Pharisee muttered to himself that if Jesus had been a prophet he would have realized that Mary was a sex worker and would have shunned her Jesus told him a story, a parable if you like:

> *There was a certain creditor who had two debtors. One owed five hundred denarii* (£25,000/$37,500) *and the other fifty denarii* (£2,500/$3,750). *And when they had nothing with which to repay, he freely forgave them both. Tell me, therefore, which of them will love him more?*

Simon naturally felt that the answer was the one who had been forgiven the greater amount. Jesus agreed with him and went on to remind Simon of all the things that as a host he had neglected to do. It would have been normal to provide water for the guests to wash off the dust from their feet and get comfortable before eating but no water had been provided. Also he had shown no warmth in his welcome. An eastern style kiss would have been normal but no kiss had been given; a dab of fragrant oil on the forehead would not have been out of place but there had been no such anointing. By contrast Mary had washed Jesus' feet with her tears and wiped them with her hair, she had covered his feet with kisses and she had anointed his feet with fragrant oil. So, as a result, Jesus says:

Her sins, which are many, are forgiven, for she loved much.

That is an astonishing statement. Because of Mary's love for Jesus, demonstrated in the washing, wiping, kissing and anointing, her sins were forgiven. In that instant all the guilt that had accumulated as a result of the misuse of her body was discharged. It was as if it had never happened. The slate was wiped clean. The books were balanced. The debt was paid off. And the burden of shame that weighed her down was lifted from her heart leaving her feeling like a new person. For the first time in years she felt clean. [5]

There is a wonderfully brief proverb in the Old Testament that is also quoted by Peter in his first letter:

Hatred stirs up strife, but love covers all sins.[6]

If, as I have argued, love is the fundamental stuff of reality then it should come as no surprise that love has the power to counter and obliterate evil. There are dreadful things going on in our world. There have always been dreadful things going on in our world. At the time of writing the prime example filling the news channels is of a terrorist massacre in a Nairobi shopping mall.

This obliterated the previous week's news about the use of nerve gas in the Syrian civil war. Next week there will be another piece of bad news dominating TV and radio and our natural reaction to such human bad behavior is to counter it with more hatred and violence. Yet the wisdom coming from Jesus is that we must deploy something completely different. We must find a way to swamp the problem with love.

Forgiveness the Icebreaker

I would be being less than honest if I pretended to understand how that would work in Kenya or Syria. I cannot imagine the train of events that could lead from an act of love to the solution of a deeply seated racial, sectarian or political problem. What I do know is that in my own life there are decision points where I can either harden or soften my attitude towards another person and more often than not the right course is to soften my attitude and make some move to demonstrate it.

In October 2007 I attended the international assembly of a charity in which I serve as a volunteer. On this occasion the venue was Sarajevo, the capital city of a country that had experienced in its fairly recent past immense human tragedy and suffering. Several local people had been invited to speak and as one would expect their experiences of losing close friends and family during the war were harrowing. One woman in particular stuck in my mind because she had lost her husband and all, I think it was three, of her sons in the Srebrnica genocide. She had rediscovered purpose for her life in campaigning to bring the perpetrators, who were still walking free, to justice. Many years after her bereavement I could still feel her agony and her anger.

In contrast were two other visitors to the conference, an Israeli and a Palestinian, who had both lost children and siblings in that particular conflict. They were developing a network of families, from both sides of the divide, who had a similar history. Their purpose was to seek reconciliation at a personal and family level through meeting and talking together. I had breakfast with the Israeli one morning and discovered a man with a caring and yet practical approach. He had compassion and commitment.

I feel great sympathy for that woman and yet I think that the two men are more likely to come up with a solution both for themselves and for their people.

Forgiveness is the icebreaker, the thin end of the wedge of love, the first step into a change of attitude. If we have been wronged then we must forgive. If we have been in the wrong then we must seek forgiveness. Forgiveness promotes love and then love produces even more forgiveness.

Faith, the Catalyst

This virtuous spiral can be seen in Jesus' words to Simon. The story of the two debtors makes the point that love is proportional to forgiveness. The man who had been forgiven the debt of £25000 loved his creditor more than the man who had been cleared of £2500. Jesus is telling us that the scale of Mary's forgiveness was reflected in the extent of her love. But Jesus is also saying that Mary was forgiven because of the love that she had demonstrated. Her love was both the cause and the result of her forgiveness.

To understand how this works we have to factor into our thinking a very important word that Jesus used: faith. He said to Mary:

> *Your sins are forgiven; your faith has saved you; go in peace.*

Faith is the perception of a reality that is hidden from the normal five senses. Faith visualizes the thing that is hoped for and gives it substance. Faith visits the spiritual realm that lies above, beyond and beneath our material realm and draws from it the direction and power to change the course of events in our physical world. Whether or not the Israeli and the Palestinian men at my conference realized it, they were exercising faith.

Jesus saw in Mary's actions evidence of faith. The washing and the anointing and the kissing were acts of love and kindness but they stemmed from something else that had already been established in Mary's life. Jesus saw that they were prompted by faith. Mary believed that she could and would be forgiven so she proceeded to act on her faith in full expectation that her forgiveness would follow in due course.

In recognizing the catalytic action of faith in this sequence of events we can see how the paradox in Jesus' words makes sense. By faith Mary's forgiveness preceded and was the motivation for her loving actions but forgiveness was also the result of, or, we might almost say, the reward for her love. Both things are true: love was both the cause and the evidence of her forgiveness.

So love is at the core of Jesus' gospel, intellectually, emotionally and physically. Love opens up the access to forgiveness, healing, restoration and peace. By giving this story such a prominent role in the proclamation of his gospel, Jesus is making it clear that love in all its aspects lies at the heart of real and fruitful living for us humans. The first and greatest commandment is that we should love the Lord our God with every fiber of our being and the second is that we should love our neighbor as our self.[7]

The Hole in the Roof

This love leads to forgiveness and forgiveness leads to healing. Forgiveness and healing are closely associated and are indeed almost synonymous in Jesus' teaching. The profession in which Mary was engaged carried serious risks to the health of both body and mind and it is highly likely that she experienced physical and psychological healing at the same time that she was forgiven. When Jesus said that her faith had saved her it would be a mistake to assume that this was purely a reference to her eternal destination; Jesus was not just talking about Mary "going to heaven when she died". Its primary meaning would have been that the damage sustained by Mary's mind and body as a result of her life as a prostitute was being repaired. She was being given a fresh start in this life.

Throughout the Gospels healing and forgiveness are closely intertwined. This is perfectly demonstrated in the story about the healing of a disabled man recorded in all three of the Synoptic Gospels.[8]

One day Jesus was in a house in Capernaum packed with a large crowd. He was teaching and healing sick people. Four men arrived carrying a man suffering from paralysis on a stretcher and being unable to get into the house because of the crowd they went up onto the roof and broke through the tiling.

At this point I find myself feeling very sorry for the owner of the house. Mark's words carry a suggestion that the house was that of Peter and Andrew, so I picture Peter's wife looking up in horror as dust and then pieces of broken tiles started falling from the ceiling until finally there was a gaping hole large enough to lower a bed through. Then I imagine Jesus, the joiner-builder, noticing the dismayed expression on her face and whispering in her ear "Don't worry. It will only take me a couple of hours to fix it when everyone has gone."

All three accounts agree that Jesus then said to the paralyzed man "Your sins are forgiven", exactly the same thing he said to Mary in the house of Simon the Pharisee. Now there were a number of religious teachers present and they took exception to Jesus doing something that they thought only God could do, that is, forgive sins. In response Jesus asked them whether it was easier to say what he had said or to tell the man to get up and walk. He then proceeded to tell the man to get up and walk and the man did just that. In so doing Jesus was making the words "forgiveness" and "healing" virtually synonymous.[9]

So in Mary's story we can find some powerful concepts that lie at the heart of Jesus' gospel. The core, the solid center to the gospel is love, multidimensional, powerful, enduring love, pictured in Mary's story as a kind of loving between a man and a woman that has moved beyond sexual intercourse into a different kind of attraction and fulfillment. Soulmate friendship and a willingness to give all that one is and has for the sake of the beloved mark the start of this spikenard love.

Such love must be channeled through faith. Mary's story tells us that faith will enable us to go out on a limb and express love in new ways to people we do not yet know, blessing them and bringing forgiveness and healing and peace to both them and ourselves.

Nicodemus

This is a powerful story and it is interesting that the New Testament does provide some evidence that in the early years of the church Mary's story was commonly known amongst the Christian community.

John, who wrote his Gospel many decades after Jesus lived, tells us in his chapter eleven about the raising of Lazarus, Mary's brother, from the dead. Chronologically this miracle preceded Mary's anointing of Jesus at Bethany, an incident that John reports in chapter twelve. Yet in chapter eleven John refers to Mary as "the woman who anointed the Lord with fragrant oil and wiped his feet with her hair". Why would he do that when he is going to tell the anointing story in the very next chapter? Some commentators say this is a prospective reference to something that had not yet been related by John but that just seems like giving the problem a name without solving it; there is still no obvious reason to employ such a device. Furthermore this would be the only prospective reference in John's Gospel. By contrast there are two clear retrospective references where John is ensuring that we have identified the right person by mentioning an earlier incident. It is worth taking a look at these in order to understand this feature of John's writing.

In chapter three John introduces us to Nicodemus, a ruler of the Jews, who comes to Jesus by night to find out more about him. Some time later, as recorded in chapter seven, Nicodemus is found defending Jesus against criticism by a group of his fellow Pharisees. John reminds us that this is the same Nicodemus that had earlier come to Jesus by night. Then in chapter nineteen Nicodemus helps Joseph of Arimathea to bury Jesus' body and again John reminds us that this was the same Nicodemus who came to Jesus by night. John wants to make sure that we know exactly whom he is talking about: Nicodemus who came to Jesus by night.

So it is a feature of John's writing that he will refer back to an earlier incident to ensure that the reader correctly identifies the person he is talking about. Against that background, John's reference to Mary's anointing of Jesus before he actually relates that particular incident could indicate that John expected his readers to be familiar with Mary's story. The case is not watertight but it does point towards Mary's story being well known at the end of the first century.

At this juncture my imagination set to work – again! It seemed likely that Jesus intended Mary's story to be told over and again as a way of helping people to understand exactly what the good news is about. There is nothing quite like a story about a real person to get people focusing on the essence of the gospel of Jesus. In fact it turns out that Mary's story is the only story that Jesus specifically said would or should be included in or with the preaching of the gospel. I have checked all the places where Jesus talks directly about the content of his gospel and there is no other story that he said should be included. All the relevant verses are listed in Appendix 4 if you wish to verify this. Mary's story stands alone in having been specifically picked out by Jesus.

Just think of some of the wonderful personal stories that fill the Gospels:

- The man called Legion, because he was possessed by so many demons, is restored to his right mind and told "Go home to your friends, and tell them what great things the Lord has done for you, and how he has had compassion on you."

- Bartimaeus, the blind beggar, is healed and told, "Go your way your faith has made you well."

- Simon Peter, moved to become a disciple of Jesus after witnessing a miraculous catch of fish, sees clearly into the state of his own heart when he says to Jesus, "Depart from me, for I am a sinful man, O Lord!"

- Zacchaeus, the repentant tax extortionist, gives away half his fortune to the poor and restores fourfold any money he had obtained falsely. Jesus tells him, "Today salvation has come to this house."

- Nicodemus is told, "Unless one is born again, he cannot see the kingdom of God." He becomes an undercover disciple of Jesus.

I have selected these particular accounts of transformed lives because they contain the person's name; there are dozens more where the lead character remains anonymous. And according to John there were hundreds more that never even got recorded.[10] Something must have stood out in Jesus' mind about Mary that made him choose her story before all the others as the ideal one to accompany the proclamation of his gospel.

Legion's exorcism tells us about God's compassion for us; Bartimaeus' healing tells us how important faith is to the working of the gospel; Peter's conversion emphasizes the need for recognition of our own unworthiness; Zacchaeus' story shows us the significance of repenting and making amends; and Nicodemus' being born again demonstrates the importance of the work of the Spirit of God inside the human heart. Yet Jesus chose none of these stories to accompany the preaching of his gospel; he chose Mary's story.

Even if I am wrong about Mary's story being one joined-up narrative, even if Mary of Bethany was not the redeemed Galilean prostitute and the spikenard had come to her by some other means, we are still left with a beautiful story of a woman so devoted to Jesus of Nazareth that the only way she could express her love was to pour £15000 worth of perfume onto his head and feet and get down on her knees and wipe his feet with her hair.

By selecting this story to accompany the preaching of his gospel Jesus is telling us that love, spikenard love, is the priority, the beginning and the end and the very heart of his message.

You could stop reading this book now. In one sense there is nothing more to say. There is enough information in these first three chapters to enable you to live better from now to the end of your days and to safeguard your eternal destiny. You could continue to be a non-believer or an agnostic or to follow the religious tradition you are familiar with while at the same time adding to your life, if they are not already installed there, the key foundational principles of Jesus' teaching. In my understanding of Jesus' gospel you would thereby secure your citizenship of the kingdom of heaven and be in good shape to face God one day.

But then again, you bought this book, so you may as well carry on reading because there is a whole lot more to Jesus' gospel. God's intention is to change the world through people like you and me and to do that he needs us, or at least some of us, to become disciples of Jesus Christ. However, I must warn you that the going gets harder from now on. This discipleship stuff is not for the fainthearted. If you are still with me then let's have a go at unpacking faith.

Chapter 4

Second Childhood

Could Jesus, God's perfect Son, ever have had an infantile temper tantrum?

My sister asked me this question some time ago when we were discussing Jesus' childhood and seemed surprised when I said that he probably did have a temper. We humans start out as babies with a hundred billion neurons and relatively few synapses. We are born with a mind that is largely unstructured, stimulated by hunger and discomfort. Engaging with our environment forms our thinking and behavior. Initially that environment consists only of our parents and our home but increasingly we take in aspects of the wider world. Progressively we learn the importance of catering for the needs of others and acquire social skills.

We develop a sense of right and wrong and of different categories of right and wrong. By the time we are at playschool we are capable of distinguishing between that which is morally wrong (e.g. deliberately hurting someone) and the lesser evil of breaking a social code (e.g. talking at the same time as the teacher). This process of acquiring knowledge and skills, learning how to think and improving our decision-making continues, ideally, for the rest of our lives.

Although followers of Christ have had various ideas about Jesus' divinity most have thought that he was human. He was the product of genes. He had parents, or at least one parent, and a chain of ancestors who were very much a part of the human race. He was born as a baby just like the rest of us. His mind was formed in the same way as is ours through observation, experience and memory. That is why I think he was just as likely as any one of us to have had a temper tantrum at some time during his infancy. But how can this be reconciled with his divinity? In this chapter I will offer a personal view that works for me. See what you think.

Research has demonstrated that young children naturally tend to believe in God. The views of Dr Justin Barrett, then a senior researcher at Oxford University's Center for Anthropology and Mind, were first reported in The Daily Telegraph in November, 2008. Based on the results of psychological experiments he concluded that young people have an inclination to believe in a Supreme Being because they assume that everything in the world was created with a purpose. [1] (There may, however, be some exceptions; Sir David Attenborough has said that it never really occurred to him to believe in God. But does his memory go back far enough?)

Like us, or most of us, Jesus would have come to believe that everything had a purpose and that there was some kind of Supreme Being behind the world that we perceive with our five senses. In his case this normal instinct for God became especially intense. By the time he was twelve he regarded God as his Father. Although all the Christians I know relate to God as their Father, Jesus came to experience and portray that relationship in a uniquely proactive way. In the life of Jesus faith grew faster and deeper than it does for the rest of us and reached into areas of life that are beyond the limits that you or I normally come up against.

Jesus Needed Faith

Faith, according to the author of the letter to the Hebrews, is the evidence of things not seen.[2] It is that which gives substance to the things for which we hope. Faith connects us to the hidden realities of existence, enabling us to explore and come to understand things that cannot be accessed directly by sight, sound, touch, taste or smell.

Jesus needed faith to be aware of God. If he really was human, completely human, then he had exactly the same set of senses and mental faculties that we have. He did not have "something extra", a spiritual implant from the eternal realm that enabled him to know God directly in a way that we regular humans are incapable of, a hotline to heaven that is absent from our makeup. Like us his knowledge of God came indirectly through his own body, mind and emotions. The information he gathered through his senses was processed in a mind formed exactly like ours but the end product was an awareness and knowledge of God far in excess of that which the rest of us ever manage to achieve.

It has taken me most of my life to grasp this fact and its consequences. There always used to be an escape hatch in my mind so that whenever I was challenged by Jesus' actions dramatically exceeding my capabilities (e.g. walking on water or healing the blind). I could slip into the thought that this was actually his divine nature working underneath, you could almost say leaking through, his humanity. It was to me as if his humanity was little more than a disguise. However, things became a whole lot clearer and also a whole lot more challenging when I took on board the full significance of Jesus' statement that his disciples would do the same works, and indeed greater works than he had done.[3] I take that to mean greater in quantity rather than quality but even matching the quality of Jesus' works seems unattainable. Yet Jesus was implying that everything he did was done as a genetic member of our race and not as God in mufti.

Even Paul struggles with this idea when trying to explain the nature of Jesus to the Christians at Philippi.[4] He says that Jesus came from the eternal realm, where he was equal with God, down to earth "in the likeness of men" and that he was "in appearance as a man". To me Paul is saying that Jesus was, in his earthly life, more than human; he only appeared to be a man. But in that case when was Jesus ever completely human, as orthodox Christian thinking has always insisted? To be completely human Jesus needed to have more than a resemblance to humanity; he needed to actually be human.

The idea of the eternally pre-existent second person of the triune God becoming incarnate in Mary's womb is deeply embedded in my thinking, just as it is hard-wired into the theology of all doctrinally orthodox Christians. But then how can Jesus actually be completely human? Let me share a possible explanation.

Sawdust and Sweat

The first important idea to grasp is that eternity, the realm of God, is not an infinitely long period of time; it is something other than, something different from, time. Picture time as a river winding through a valley with humans drifting on rafts along the current. We can remember the stretch of water that represents the lifespan over which we have traveled. We also have reports and records of earlier periods handed down to us from others who lived before us, but we have no paddle or motor that will enable us to go back upstream and we have only very limited ability to anticipate the stretch ahead of us. We are only fully aware of and able to live on the part of the river where we are, that is in the present.

Cosmologists think that time came into existence along with space, matter and energy, at the inception of the universe. Eternity is a different kind of domain altogether. In eternity change is measured against some dimension other than time, something different from the process of decay that underpins our experience of time. So, in this picture, God can be likened to the pilot of a helicopter flying overhead, able not only to see but also, most importantly, to visit all points along the river. Anyone living in eternity is not bound by time and is universally present at all times.

Now add a further twist to the picture. Imagine Jesus as the first and so far the only human to have been winched up off his raft on the river of time to sit alongside the helicopter pilot in eternity. This resurrected and transformed human ascends into God's realm and can thus see and visit all parts of the river. The entire span of time including its source and its ending is both visible and, most importantly, accessible and tangible to him.

He can be the architect of creation and the Lamb slain from the foundation of the world. He can be the eternal Word made flesh that dwelt among us. He can also drop in at any point in our time dimension before or after the earthly life of the carpenter of Nazareth as, for example, Melchizedek who blessed Abraham, or the person Saul of Tarsus encountered on the Damascus Road. He can do all of those things and still be a fully integrated member of the human race who only existed as a genetic possibility until a fertilized ovum began its unique journey in Mary's womb.

The idea that God picked out Jesus, a regular human, and transformed him into the second person of the Godhead is called Adoptionism and it has cropped up from time to time throughout the history of the church, generally being regarded as heretical. If you are picturing eternity as an infinitely long period of time, and I suspect most of us start there because we struggle to imagine a timeless domain, then it follows that Adoptionism denies the pre-existent divine person who became Jesus. Basically it would be saying that God did not have a Son until Jesus came along and it should be rightly dismissed as a heterodox idea. But for me the winding river and helicopter picture of time and eternity closes the loop; it resolves the paradox of how Jesus can be both completely human in his earthly existence and completely God in eternity.

Scary, isn't it? Jesus, the man, is so human that if I had been with him in his workshop I would have been able to smell the sweat and the sawdust on his shirt and see him become physically and mentally tired from his labor. Yet he has pioneered a new kind of humanity that can make the transition into God's eternal realm. Jesus stands at the pinnacle of our God-inspired human development. In Jesus the life of the Creator fully connects with the creation. God acquires a body of flesh and a human becomes divine. And because of the relationship between time and eternity, the river and the helicopter, there is a human with God, indeed there is a human side of God, throughout the entire domain of eternity.

Becoming as Little Children

Against that background let us return to exploring how we, like Jesus, can come to understand and practice faith as humans without any additional "superhuman" senses or powers. According to Justin Barrett, the greater part of scientific evidence over the past ten years or so has shown that much more seems to be built into the natural development of children's minds than we once thought, including an inclination, an instinctive bias, to see the natural world as designed and purposeful and that some kind of intelligent being is behind that purpose. Young children have faith even when family or school has not taught them about faith.

Now this does not, of course, prove that the natural world is designed and purposeful or that there is an intelligent being behind the scenes. However, it does give us a very good reason to explore the nature of faith.

Jesus clearly understood this awareness of young children as can be seen from the following account, compiled from Matthew, Mark and Luke, of an incident, that possibly took place in Peter's house and perhaps featured Peter's child:

> *Then he came to Capernaum. And when he was in the house he asked them, "What was it you disputed among yourselves on the road?" But they kept silent, for on the road they had disputed among themselves who would be the greatest.*
>
> *And Jesus, perceiving the thought of their heart, took a little child and set him by him. And when he had taken him in his arms, he said to them, "Assuredly, I say to you, unless you are converted*

> *and become as little children, you will by no means enter the kingdom of heaven. Therefore whoever humbles himself as this little child is the greatest in the kingdom of heaven.*
>
> *"Whoever receives one of these little children in my name receives me; and whoever receives me, receives not me but him who sent me. But whoever causes one of these little ones who believe in me to sin, it would be better for him if a millstone were hung around his neck, and he were drowned in the depth of the sea."*[5]

In a separate later incident, also recorded in all three Synoptic Gospels, the disciples, who appear not to have understood what Jesus had said to them on that previous occasion in Capernaum, were rebuking people who were bringing their children to Jesus so that he might touch them.

> *But when Jesus saw it, he was greatly displeased and said to them, "Let the little children come to me, and do not forbid them; for of such is the kingdom of God. Assuredly, I say to you, whoever does not receive the kingdom of God as a little child will by no means enter it."*[6]

What Justin Barrett and Jesus are saying dovetail beautifully together. Young children instinctively feel that the world has meaning and purpose because there is some kind of Supreme Being behind it. To enter into that domain of faith, which comes so naturally to the very young, it is necessary for adults to become like little children, to be converted (literally "to turn") from adult ways of thinking and rediscover the freshness and directness of approach to God that is so characteristic of young children.

Forbidden Fruit

This is not to reject all the knowledge that we have gained and all the useful things that human ingenuity has produced. Jesus had extensive knowledge of the world around him and made use of the technologies that were available to him. Even though on one occasion he walked on water, most of the time he made use of the boat builder's skills to cross the Sea of Galilee. And as a carpenter he would have needed the art of the blacksmith to supply him with his tools. Science and technology have progressed since Jesus' day but we can and should still welcome their ability to enrich our lives.

It is only when we see knowledge and invention in some way as substitutes for God that we run into trouble. Let us revisit the story of Adam and Eve to see how God intended us to run our lives and how it has gone so badly wrong.

There was only one rule in the Garden of Eden. It concerned the fruit of the tree of knowledge of good and evil. This was the only tree whose fruit was not to be eaten. Now I need to point out, because sometimes speakers and writers overlook this, that it was specifically the knowledge of good and evil that was off-limits to the first humans. Knowledge in general was not forbidden, only knowledge of good and evil, or, as we would say, wisdom. God retained that particular realm of knowledge for himself. Whenever a tough question arose as to which was the correct choice between two alternatives God was on hand to supply the necessary guidance.

Every day God answered their questions and introduced them to new and exciting ideas. Evidently God was in the habit of taking an early morning walk in the garden where he would meet with Adam and Eve for a debriefing on the previous day and a chat about the day ahead. Each morning they could look forward to fresh opportunities, places to go, things to do, and, after a bit of enjoyable breeding time, people to meet. It was very important, however, that they depended entirely upon God to supply all the wisdom they needed. As long as they held to that course then everything would be fine but if they ever tried to substitute their own judgment then they would enter a downward spiral that would eventually destroy them. Sadly, however, they disobeyed the only rule imposed upon them:

So when the woman saw that the tree was good for food, that it was pleasant to the eyes, and a tree desirable to make one wise, she took its fruit and ate. She also gave to her husband with her, and he ate.[7]

In eating the forbidden fruit Adam and Eve were prompted by two distinct motives and were simultaneously making two different kinds of mistake. On the one hand they gave themselves a visual and gourmet treat and slipped into self-gratification; they saw that the fruit was pleasant to the eyes and good for food and they became slaves to sensuality. On the other hand they sought direct access to wisdom as if wisdom were some kind of commodity that could exist apart from the Creator. Such independent imitation wisdom can only be based on, and therefore limited by, past experience. It results in legalism, living by a set of rules based on history, whereas Divine wisdom with its much greater ability to foresee the future consequences of choices made in the present is of a far higher order.

On the one hand the tree was desirable because it would make them wise, like God they would understand good and evil. On the other hand there was an attraction to something that was visually pleasing and good to eat. As I reflect on our human tendency to make a mess of our lives it seems to me that these are still the main pressures that mold and mar our choices. The obsession with being in control of our future and the desire to enjoy ourselves at almost any cost are exactly the same primary temptations we struggle with.

Real Wisdom

Take first our desire for wisdom. Human wisdom is based upon past experience and a very limited ability to anticipate or forecast the future. We draw on our personal history and the knowledge we have gained from talking to others or reading about their experiences in order to make choices in the present that will have consequences in the future. When things work out well we pride ourselves on our prudence and foresight; when the outcome is less successful we put it down to bad luck. In reality, though, we can do little more than prepare ourselves for what may or may not happen.

Life is uncertain. Yes, there are a large number of events that happen with sufficient regularity that we regard them for all practical purposes as certain. The rising of the sun has a pattern that enables us to predict the precise moment at which it will appear over the horizon at any particular place in the world on any given day. Fortunately for us there are many other features of our world that behave like that; life would be extremely difficult if that were not the case. And yet when we strip the world back to its fundamental constituents it transpires that there is nothing actually certain at all.

So uncertainty, even though we are not necessarily always conscious of it, has become deeply embedded in our collective psyche. We have become preoccupied with not repeating the mistakes of the past. Typically our worries get codified into some form of rule that is expressed either as "thou shalt" or as "thou shalt not" and in this way we build up a regulatory framework that defines right and wrong behavior. At a personal or family level there are many informal codes of conduct and in our larger society the most important, or perhaps the most politically pressing, become laws of the land.

God did not intend us to function this way. He did not give Adam and Eve a rulebook to follow. There was only one rule: just leave it to God to sort out. His plan was for us to draw directly on his wisdom. There was to be no need for us to have independent understanding of right and wrong in matters of personal morality, business dealings, family affairs, social justice or any other area of human thought and action. We should be able to access all the wisdom we need at the point of decision directly from the Divine mind. Since God is able to foresee the outcome of our choices far better than we can, the quality of wisdom available to us is vastly greater than the alternative human substitute wisdom based solely on past experience.

So, one intention in God's ban on eating the fruit of the tree of knowledge of good and evil was to protect us from substituting inferior human wisdom for directly accessible Divine wisdom. His other purpose was to prevent us from becoming slaves to our physical and emotional appetites.

Self- Control

Eve saw, and persuaded Adam, that as well as making them smart the fruit looked good and was delicious. When they ate it they realized that they were naked and made coverings for themselves. Who did they need to hide their bodies from? God and each other it seems. That which until then had been unconsciously part of who they were suddenly became intrusive and needing to be controlled. The simple joy of togetherness became a desire for pleasure as an end in itself and they became trapped in a futile cycle of events, driven by the need to satisfy appetites that are actually insatiable.

So, on the one hand we experiment unwisely with material things and substances and behavior patterns that do us no good and enslave us; and on the other hand we multiply the creation of rules and regulations to curb our innate tendency to waywardness and a chaotic lifestyle. However, between the paralyzing demands and restrictions of law and the chaotic and binding results of self-indulgence there is a path of equilibrium where we can enjoy real freedom. For Adam and Eve that path was defined by obedience to God in the matter of the forbidden fruit. Everything else was unrestricted to them. They could go anywhere in the garden and eat the fruit of all the other trees.

When Adam and Eve disobeyed God on the one crucial point

they simultaneously became the slaves of both law and passion. On the one hand they became locked into a very inferior form of wisdom based upon past experience and on the other they became unable to control their sensuality. The most important consequence of this was that they were banished from the garden and denied access to the tree of life, the tree that preserved them from disease and death.[8] They became prone to sickness of body and mind. They became mortal. Theologically this alienation from God is known as The Fall.

So the Garden of Eden story conveys a highly relevant truth about how and why we humans screw up the way we do and in its light Jesus' emphasis on the importance of becoming like little children takes on a fuller meaning. The age of innocence needs to be recaptured. Simple dependence on a heavenly Father needs to be re-established in our lives. Our knowledge and our cleverness are not to be abandoned but need to be set in their rightful place under the government of God so that his authority is exercised through the willing submission of our own wisdom to that of our Creator.

We can trace this pathway in Mary's story. She was trapped inside her profession. There was no hope for her to ever break free from prostitution, yet that was what she wanted to do with all her heart. Whether she had previously met Jesus, as I have suggested in my reconstruction, or whether she had only heard about him or seen him in a crowd we do not know but when she found out that he was dining with Simon the Pharisee a plan formed in her mind. She headed for Simon's house with a flask of fragrant oil.

She took an enormous risk in standing at Jesus' feet weeping so that her tears were dripping onto his feet. That prompted the next step. She got down on her knees and began to wash his feet with her tears. Then she dried them with her hair. Just imagine all this. Picture in your mind the drama and the emotion of this moment. In wiping his feet with her hair her face would have been down on a level with his feet so she kissed them. Then she took out the flask and anointed his feet with the fragrant oil. She had gone out on a limb and only Jesus could rescue her from the situation. The normal reaction that such a public display by a prostitute would have provoked was revulsion and rejection. She was longing for something better than that from Jesus. This was faith in action.

What Is Faith?

Including Mary's story there are twenty-one passages in the Synoptic Gospels where Jesus speaks about the subject of "faith" or "believing". (In New Testament Greek those two words are from the same stem and look very similar.) There is a complete list in Appendix 5 but here is a brief synopsis.

Twelve of the cases demonstrate faith in action. People are healed of paralysis, fever, hemorrhage, blindness, demon possession, epilepsy, leprosy and catalepsy. A storm is stilled, water becomes solid enough to walk on and a prostitute's life is transformed. The twelfth case demonstrates how unbelief, lack of faith, prevents good things from happening.

Then there are eight passages in which Jesus teaches about faith. He tells us we can have little or no faith and that faith can be increased but can also fail. He tells us that little children naturally believe and we must become like them if we are to enter the kingdom of God. He tells us that faith is receiving the word of God into our heart and, dispelling all doubt, firmly establishing in our mind that we will get what we pray for. Finally he intimates that "when the Son of Man comes" faith will be in short supply on the earth.

So, there we have twenty of the twenty-one passages. The odd one out is Mark 16:14-18. Here Jesus is reported as saying that believing or not believing in his resurrection will determine whether one is saved or condemned. This idea appears nowhere else in the Synoptic Gospels and virtually all scholars agree that this passage was added at a later date. John's Gospel, written later than the Synoptic Gospels, contains much of this kind of thinking. John openly acknowledges that he is adding to the history of Jesus, the man, ideas that could only have been developed after his glorification. [9] Of course, it is vitally important for Christians to believe in the divine nature of Jesus but we need to separate the two pictures because only the human Jesus can show us how to live as humans. To learn how to be people of faith, hope and love in this life we should focus on Jesus the man.

Faith (or believing) is a flexible idea and it has a spectrum of meanings. At one end of the spectrum it means holding in ones mind as indubitably true certain items of information that cannot be rigorously proven. The supreme example of this is that the resurrection of Jesus actually happened. At the other end of the spectrum faith is about simply trusting God for everything. The first is faith in the mind; the second is faith in the heart. John in his Gospel tends to dwell on the first kind of meaning, often calling for belief in Jesus' divinity, whereas the Synoptic Gospels present faith, almost exclusively, in the second sense.

Reversing the Fall

In Matthew, Mark and Luke, time and again, Jesus shows us that the way to reverse the effects of the Fall is to become as little children. We must return to a simple acceptance that God is behind all the events of our lives and that he has good purposes for us and everyone else. Things may not always look as if they are good and right and there are endless opportunities for us to make them better or worse but we will most effectively enter into the creative and healing process if we acknowledge God as supremely and benignly in control. In this way we can mitigate and reverse the effects of the "sickness" that blights every area of our lives and we can unscramble the mess that we tend to get into when we reject the wisdom of God and follow our own self-gratifying desires.

This kind of faith does not require our intellectual acceptance of any particular set of ideas or body of information or religious doctrine. It is not an ideology, a worldview or a belief system. It is a childlike dependence on God and a willingness to seek him out and follow his leading. The kingdom of heaven is composed of people who do this and those who do it best, says Jesus, are the ones who carry the greatest authority in the kingdom of God. The more we come to regard ourselves as and behave like the little children of our heavenly Father that in reality we are then the more we will experience of God's life and power and love flowing through us. Paradoxically, as we become more like children we become more like warriors, able to wield God's authority against the evil in our world.

When Mary the prostitute came to Jesus she was not casting herself on the person who had died on the cross for her sins or who had been declared to be the Son of God with power by his rising from the dead because neither of those things had happened. Mary came to Jesus because she recognized him as a man with whom God was present in a remarkably powerful way. He knew God and the ways of God to an extent that marked him out as one possessing an uncommon relationship with God and therefore as one who could help others to find the way to God. To some lesser degree we can follow that same path and become beacons directing others to the kingdom of heaven. We can become less and less a part of the problem and increasingly a part of the solution.

This childlike faith needs to be applied in several areas of our lives if we are to be trained and equipped for this work. First of all restoration is needed because, unlike Jesus, we have a record of failure to be put right. We have a history of ignoring God's wisdom and gratifying our selfish desires. There are impediments from the past that weigh us down. These things must be dealt with if we are to become fully effective servants of the King.

God must deal first with our own history and personal baggage. We will explore how the Holy Spirit does this in the next chapter.

Chapter 5

Renewed Minds

In his 2006 book *The God Delusion,* Richard Dawkins describes a case study in the roots of morality.[1] This draws upon some psychological research into the moral sense of real people carried out by the Harvard biologist Marc Hauser using questionnaires on the Internet. One of Hauser's thought experiments imagines a person, Denise, standing by a railway line, close to a set of points that she can operate to divert a runaway trolley onto a siding, thereby saving the lives of five people trapped on the main line ahead. Unfortunately there is also one other person trapped on the siding who will die instead of the five who will be saved.

The participants in the experiment were asked to decide whether switching the points was morally "obligatory", "permissible" or "forbidden". In the event ninety percent of people said it was permissible to divert the trolley, killing the one to save the five, and there was no statistically significant difference between atheists and religious believers in making this judgment. From this and the results of similar experiments Richard Dawkins concludes:

> *This seems compatible with the view that we do not need God in order to be good – or evil.* (Richard Dawkins. *The God Delusion*)

Dawkins' conclusion is, of course, erroneous. What the experiment shows is that we do not need to BELIEVE in God in order to be good. It proves nothing about our need of God. Thankfully it is indeed the case that the moral law is universal and operates across national, cultural and religious boundaries. It is independent of beliefs. When faced with a tough but clearly defined moral choice most of us know instinctively the right way to go. The really interesting question to ask is why this should be so. Why is it that humans throughout all geographical and historical domains have carried remarkably similar internalized ideas about what ought and ought not to be done? C S Lewis addressed this question in his book *Mere Christianity* and concluded that the phenomenon of a universal moral law points strongly to both the existence and the character of God. More recently Francis Collins has revisited Lewis' argument in *The Language of God*.[2] But what about those decisions that have to be made when the issues are not so clear?

What would have happened if Denise had known the person trapped on the siding? What if they had been a friend or a close family member?

A few years ago on my travels in South Wales I passed through the town of Aberfan and found myself vividly recalling the shock and horror I felt on 21st October, 1966 when I heard on the radio that one hundred and sixteen children and twenty-eight adults had been buried alive in a coal mining slag heap that had suddenly collapsed. Rainwater trapped inside the mound had caused it to become unstable and a massive landslide had engulfed the local primary school.

The official enquiry blamed the National Coal Board for extreme negligence in that there was a complete absence of a tipping policy. However, the report rejected claims from the relatives of the victims of callous indifference. "Not villains, but decent men, led astray by foolishness or by ignorance or by both in combination, are responsible for what happened at Aberfan."[3]

Who among us can claim never to have acted in foolishness or ignorance?

True Genius

What causes us to fail? Why do we screw up? Why do we drift off course, perhaps imperceptibly at first but with ever increasing deviation, until our position becomes powerless and hopeless? It all comes down to the choices we make. Every day each of us makes hundreds, probably thousands of decisions. Many of them are trivial but some are huge. Most of them have no serious ramifications; they form the essential fabric of the freedom we have been granted to live and enjoy our lives as we wish. Some, however, have great potential to harm or benefit us or other people. These are the choices we need to get right. They are the watersheds in our lives. Let us call these the critical decisions.

It is important to realize that at the time many of these critical decisions are being made we do not actually have any awareness of their consequences. Sometimes the possible outcomes are staring us in the face but often we cannot see the knock-on effects for ourselves or for others. Choosing between good and evil or choosing the lesser of two evils may not actually be the most difficult decision. Toughest of all can be the choice between two things, neither apparently bad, but where the consequences are unforeseeable.

Winston Churchill once observed that,

> *True genius resides in the capacity for evaluating uncertain, hazardous and conflicting information.*[4] (*The Quotable Churchill.* Running Press)

I imagine he was referring to the kinds of situation that perpetually confronted him as the Prime Minister of a nation at war. However, this skill is constantly required in day-to-day circumstances that require us to exercise judgment. Frequently we must make important choices based on imperfect data or grapple with complex ideas surrounded by uncertainty to reach a necessary conclusion, and often the penalties for getting it wrong are severe, either for us or for others.

Jesus of Nazareth has demonstrated a full measure of true genius in getting all his critical decisions right. In doing so he has established a vital benchmark for life in the kingdom of heaven. Now that it has been shown to be possible for one human to live rightly as a child of God then potentially that way of living can become universal. That is God's goal, but he intends to reach it without violating our free will. That needs us to emulate Jesus.

So how did Jesus get all his critical decisions correct? I reckon he learned how to do it. He himself did as he taught us to do. He was not telling us to do one thing while he himself followed a completely different pathway. He taught us what he had discovered in the school of life and the most fundamental principle of the kingdom of heaven that Jesus spoke about is the need for repentance.

Repentance – Metanoia – A Change of Mind

From that time Jesus began to preach and to say, "Repent, for the kingdom of heaven is at hand."[5]

If you start reading the New Testament from the beginning of Matthew then these are the first publicly uttered words of Jesus that you will come across. Repentance is the headline message of Jesus' teaching and a major theme running through the Synoptic Gospels. Jesus said he had come to call sinners to repentance; he upbraided the cities of Chorazin and Bethsaida, where most of his mighty works had been done, because they did not, unlike ancient Nineveh, repent; he said there is joy in heaven over one sinner who repents; and he commissioned his disciples to go on preaching until repentance and forgiveness of sins had been proclaimed to all nations.[6]

Most of us become aware of the need to make changes in our lives whenever we honestly do a self-appraisal. We would understand the words "I repent" to mean something along the lines of "I feel sorrow and regret about my actions and resolve not to continue in wrong doing" and that is the main sense in which Jesus uses the word in the passages quoted above and elsewhere in the Synoptic Gospels. Any progress towards being a better person must start from such a perception and commitment.

The Greek word here translated as "repent" means, "I change my mind" or "I change the inner person". It consists of two parts and both have found their way into the English language. The first part, *meta* appears in words such as *metamorphosis* (change of form) and *metaphor* (change of meaning). The second part, *nous,* means *mind* and we use it to represent the intellect or sometimes just plain common sense. So, the word formed by putting the two parts together means "a change of mind".

The word "repentance" does not appear in Mary's story but I think it is revealed in her actions; her bringing of a flask of fragrant oil, her coming to Jesus, the tears, the washing, wiping, kissing and anointing all point to a woman who was undergoing a major upheaval in her thinking and emotions. Since the gospel that Jesus commissioned his disciples to preach was "repentance and the remission of (liberation from) sins" we can infer from the fact that Jesus said her sins were forgiven that Mary had indeed repented.

Repentance can be seen as the response of humility to the inner voice of conviction. Repentance is the process of rethinking and relearning and being renewed in the mind. It is, as Jesus said, turning to rediscover the freshness and simplicity of the little child that lives inside us.

Inner Peace

It seems to me that when Jesus talked about repentance he was teaching us that which he had experienced himself. He was not emphasizing the importance of acting in a way that he himself had never had to do but he was sharing something that he had discovered to be true in his own life. He was dealing with a subject that for him was not just theoretical; it was experimental.

As Jesus was completely human it must follow that he was speaking from experience.

However, that would appear to contradict the biblical statement that he was tempted in all points as we are but without sin.[7] I think we will find the answer to this paradox by taking a closer look at how we get into sin. If one day we find ourselves in deep moral trouble or if we have arrived by our own actions at a seriously dangerous situation then there is a clear need for repentance. But we need to think back over the sequence of events that led us to that condition if we are to learn from the experience.

Imagine yourself driving along a motorway and consider the process of steering your car. Provided you keep your eyes on the road your brain usually takes care of the job without you needing to think too much about it but actually you are continually correcting very slight course deviations. A motorcar will not steer in a straight line without constant adjustment from the driver. In a sense you are continually repenting. In all of life a similar process applies. We need to attend to the start of any meandering in our lives if we are to stay clear of sin and make a positive contribution to the kingdom of God.

I think Jesus was totally in control of himself. As he navigated his way through life he was, like us, constantly presented with new situations that required choices to be made. His fellowship with the Father, through the Holy Spirit, was such that even the slightest inclination towards a choice that had potentially negative consequences immediately caused a glitch in his inner sense of peace and the decision would then be modified as necessary. In other words he was continually repenting and continually being guided by the Holy Spirit.

Jesus told Mary: "Your sins are forgiven... your faith has saved you... Go in peace." When sin is dealt with and faith is established then peace takes over. If we start to deviate from our proper course then the first indication will be a loss of peace. It was this inner sense of peace that enabled Jesus to be alerted to and to evaluate each and every one of life's critical decisions and get them absolutely spot-on perfect. By this means he managed to keep his life accurately on course and any necessary adjustments were very small; most of the time the critical choices would have been dealt with in seconds. The method in each case, though, was the same: visualize the range of possibilities, make a provisional mental selection and seek feedback from the Holy Spirit using the peace test. Make an adjustment in the light of that feedback and check again for confirmation.

Sin, Righteousness and Judgment

During the Last Supper Jesus spoke about the ministry of the coming Holy Spirit and in particular he explained that the Spirit would convict the world of three things: sin, righteousness and judgment.[8] This is an enigmatic statement that even Jesus' own explanation does not entirely clarify but I am going to adopt these three words – sin, righteousness and judgment – as a progression of pegs on which to hang some ideas. In truth I do not think my little scheme is too far off the mark, but please judge for yourselves.

The first peg, the first area the Holy Spirit tackles in our lives, is sin. At its most basic level repentance is about facing up to and correcting those gross moral failures, biblically called "sins" that result from the violation of the Ten Commandments or their contemporary derivatives. Jesus often spoke about the big three distracting and ultimately corrupting influences on the human heart: power, sex and wealth.[9] On one occasion he expanded these three concepts into fourteen specific actions and attitudes:

- Evil thoughts
- Adulteries (sex by a married person other than with their spouse)
- Fornications (promiscuous sex, literally with prostitutes)

- Murders
- Thefts
- Covetousness (greed and the entire disregard of the rights of others)
- Wickedness (maliciousness)
- Deceit (treachery)
- Licentiousness (conduct shocking to public decency)
- Evil eye (see Matthew 6:22,23)
- Blasphemy (using abusive or scurrilous language about someone)
- Pride (haughtiness or arrogance)
- Foolishness
- False witness (telling lies about another person)[10]

To begin and to maintain our walk with God we must face up to and deal with such issues in our lives. Why not run a self-check right now and do what is necessary by way of repentance and restitution. In my own experience it is impossible to make any further progress in the spiritual life until sins like these have been dealt with. The Holy Spirit will lead us no further until we have responded to conviction of sin. When we have done that we are ready for what is hanging on the second peg.

When the Spirit has brought about our repentance over such gross moral failures he goes on to convict us of righteousness. Let us visit Jesus' ideas about righteousness as they are recorded in the rich collection of teaching that Matthew has gathered in chapters five, six and seven of his Gospel around one particular occasion on a mountain.

Character Versus Charisma

To all those present Jesus painted a picture of what the kingdom of God is going to be like. Imagine a world in which humility and meekness are dominant features, where nobody is without someone to comfort them in a time of sorrow, where mercy is extended to all and peace is universal. Picture a world in which you can safely assume that the other person is pure and honest because character is more highly prized than charisma; a world in which hostile thoughts are not harbored and reconciliation is sought without delay; a world where promises are never lightly given and always kept. In such a world marriage would be sacred, tit-for-tat behavior would be non-existent and nobody would jump on other people's failures or criticize their faults. Nobody would act aggressively, or need to. Nobody would be left impoverished because there would be no selfish hoarding of wealth and because if anyone did ask for help then they would be genuine. Forgiveness would always be granted and hypocrisy unheard of.

I think it is important to recognize there were two distinct audiences on the hill that day: there was the crowd and there were the disciples. The disciples came to Jesus but he did not dismiss the crowd and at the end of his teaching they were still there and astonished at what they had heard. So Jesus delivered this message to his disciples while permitting others to listen in.

To the people in general Jesus was saying, "This is the objective – a perfect world." To his disciples in particular Jesus was saying, "This is how it is going to come about – this is the plan." He was telling them that they were going to be the means whereby it actually happened. They were going to be the prophetic catalyst, the salt that brings out the flavor in the world, their works of power and love the light that inspires all humankind to glorify God.

Jesus said that in order for this to happen we must be perfect as our Father in heaven is perfect. He made it clear that this perfection would not come about by working through endless self-diagnostic lists of do's and don'ts. He said he had come to fulfill the law by enabling his followers to attain a degree of righteousness that exceeded the righteousness of the scribes and Pharisees. The righteousness of these religious leaders was defined by scrupulous obedience to the minutiae of Old Testament laws. Jesus said these people would be called great in the kingdom of heaven, presumably by folk who were impressed by that kind of dedication, but in actual fact they would not even make it over the threshold of God's kingdom. To be perfect is not a matter of ticking all the righteous boxes.

Perfect as Your Father in Heaven

The wisdom of God is on hand, through the indwelling Holy Spirit, to enable us to achieve a standard of righteousness that in some sense matches the perfection of our Father in heaven. I find it hard to get my head around that thought but it must be possible for us to get the critical decisions in our lives absolutely correct and become active contributors to the extension of the kingdom of heaven. We will not achieve this by rigorously following some religious system but by tuning our inner ear to the voice of God's Spirit. One thought that helps me grasp this idea of goodness, a concept that inspires me and encourages me in pursuit of the perfection of God, is that we should become perfect in the same way that God is perfect. I believe God is good not because he has no other option but because he chooses to be good. Now that kind of behavior, choosing to pursue righteousness, we can aspire to. Even though it is clearly impossible for us to ever be completely good as God is, yet we can still be good in the same way that God is good.

To stay on this track we need to remember that there is but one basic error we can make and that is to fail to rely on God to supply us with the wisdom needed to successfully manage each and every day. If we neglect this then subtle areas of shortcoming in our attitudes and actions will start to manifest themselves. Things like prejudice, envy, criticism, resentment, self-pity, pride, self-seeking, irritability, self-indulgence, anxiety, self-consciousness and insensitivity will begin to creep into our lives and tarnish our behavior. These are warnings to us.

The Aramaic and Greek words that are most commonly used respectively in the Old and New Testaments to represent the idea of "sin" both mean, literally, "missing the mark". They are the words that would be used of an archer whose arrow falls short or flies wide of the target. When we find ourselves missing the mark, when our peace is leaving us and our attitudes start to turn sour, then we can be sure it is because we have neglected the Spirit of God.

God deals with us as individuals and he has a different agenda for each one of us. If we are open to God he will take the initiative. In my experience Father deals with just one thing at a time in my life. Something will cause me to realize that I am drifting off course. When I have faced it and taken the necessary corrective action, when I have repented, he will lead me on to the next step.

As we walk this path of instant repentance then we will become righteous. This is not self-righteousness for we will be largely unconscious of self or the effect we are having or the impression we are creating. We will experience a general sense of peace and well-being and a genuine concern for the needs of others while being very much aware that we are a work-in-progress. Yet from time to time we will hear the music of heaven and feel that we are part of the choir or the orchestra. The Holy Spirit will be doing his work of convicting us of righteousness.

Lifetime Goals

All of this is to train us for judgment, the third peg, the final level of conviction and repentance. Jesus said that the coming of the Holy Spirit would signal the judgment of the ruler of this world. I take that to mean that God's authority is to be re-established over the affairs of this world, supplanting the authority of the evil one who has held sway since Adam and Eve were ejected from the Garden of Eden.

When we reach this level we will, by and large, be on top of the business of correcting errors in our own character and behavior. Although far from perfect we will know how to stay on track with God. We will be ready to move on to making choices that have enormous potential to influence the lives of other people. We will be equipped to decide between the good and the very best. We will be able to add significantly to the sum of happiness in the world and to take effective action against evil. We will be active and productive servants of God. At this level of repentance we will be in company with Jesus. We can never attain Jesus' level of harmony with God but we will be playing in the same team. We will be moving towards the key goal or goals for our life here on earth. We will be positively extending the rule of God over our planet. We will be finding our purpose, the reason why we are here and in doing so we will be following in Jesus' footsteps.

It is important to understand that Jesus' personal journey had a key goal, an ultimate purpose. All his experiences of learning to follow the Father were leading him to a culmination. And the climax to his life involved a huge critical decision and an enormous step of faith but out of it came a comprehensive spiritual victory with cosmic impact. Let us follow the final stages of Jesus' journey as he approached his lifetime goal.

The story can best be traced from the day when Peter, James and John accompanied Jesus to the top of a high mountain. Suddenly Jesus was completely transformed in his appearance. His clothes became dazzling white and his face shone like the sun. Two figures from the distant past appeared, Moses and Elijah. These were men whose dead bodies had never been found. In Moses' case the Bible says that God buried him, but Elijah took off to heaven in a fiery chariot before the eyes of his apprentice Elisha. Jesus was already thinking about his own end when this meeting took place. His walk with God had been closer even than Moses and Elijah, even closer than Enoch who one day walked with God straight into heaven! He must have been hoping that the Father was planning a similar exit strategy for him. Yet as the weeks went by the prospect of dying became ever more real to him.

In tandem with these thoughts, Jesus was increasingly coming to believe that his own death was going to open up the way for countless other humans to be released from the power of sin and death. As he ate what was to be his final Passover supper with his disciples he took bread, blessed it and broke it and gave them to eat with the words, "this is my body." Then he took a cup of wine and told them to drink it because:

> *This is my blood of the new covenant, which is shed for many for the remission of (liberation from) sins.*[11]

Twelve Legions of Angels

As Jesus had progressively developed in his faith and learned the proper use of his free will in finding and flowing with the purposes of God he had come to understand that his life was moving towards a specific destiny that had implications for the whole of humankind. God had been working towards this goal throughout the entire history of the universe and the development of the human race. Thousands of years elapsed before a person emerged who had the potential to finish the job. Finally there came onto the scene a human who learned how to be perfectly tuned into God. A man had appeared who was willing to allow the will of God to be done in and through his actions without any intervention by the Creator to overrule the freedom of his mind. It was Jesus' unconstrained choice to allow God to have total direction over his life. He had complete freedom to deny God that access but he chose to subordinate his freedom to the leading of the Spirit of God.

The supreme test was his willingness to die, because as a perfect human he had earned the right to be directly translated into the eternal realm. He had, like Elijah, hit the immortality jackpot. He could, like Enoch, have walked straight into heaven. However, if he had taken the fast track into eternal life he would have failed the ultimate test of his willingness to subjugate his own will to that of God. The only way he could succeed in this was to accept death, even though he could have by-passed it.

Peter, James and John had been present with Jesus at the raising of Lazarus as well as the mount of transfiguration, so when Jesus asked them to accompany him into the garden called Gethsemane he must have expected them to have some empathy with the anguish of mind he was going through. Jesus had demonstrated to them his power over death in cases of other people who had died and he had been honored before their eyes by Elijah, a man who had not only raised dead people but had avoided his own death altogether. Yet here Jesus was becoming increasingly convinced that he was going to have to die.

We are not told the content of his prayers in Gethsemane beyond the bottom line:

> *Father, if it is your will, remove this cup from me; nevertheless not my will, but yours, be done.*[12]

However, we can make a pretty good guess at God's answer in that a few minutes later he told the disciples:

> *Do you think that I cannot now pray to my Father, and he will provide me with more than twelve legions of angels?*[13]

Jesus could have opted out. There must have been enormous pressure on him to summon those angels and the fiery chariot. The writer to the Hebrews says of this agonizing experience that Jesus,

> *Offered up prayers and supplications, with vehement cries and tears to him who was able to save him from death, and was heard because*

of his godly fear, though he was a Son, yet he learned obedience through the things which he suffered.[14]

In the midst of intense mental suffering, Jesus took this his final and most important step of obedience to the leading of the Spirit of God.

The Crisis of History

If Jesus had succumbed to the temptation and backed out then God's Master Plan would have been in ruins, the whole patient build-up from Adam to Jesus would have been negated and the entire enterprise would have had to go back to the drawing board.

Luke tells us that an angel came and strengthened Jesus. I fancy I can hear that quiet reassuring voice: "Jesus, it's your decision. The Father is not compelling you to do this. If you feel that it is too much to bear then say the word and I am authorized to come with twelve legions of angels to rescue you right now. God will love you just the same. Nobody is going to blame you if you choose not to go through with this. Yet think of the immense blessing that will be achieved for the whole of your race if you can steel yourself and finish the task you have so admirably performed so far and reach the goal you have been preparing for throughout your life. God needs you to carry on trusting him."

Thankfully for us he did not give way to temptation, and the crisis of human history was faced and dealt with in those three hours. This, the toughest of all Jesus' decisions resulted in him taking up his cross, literally. He could have called for the angels. Instead he took the ultimate step of self-denial that led to his shouldering a Roman gibbet and dragging it up the hill of Calvary to his own execution. And this act of faith and obedience changed the world.[15]

The wonderful thing is that after the horror of the cross and the power of the Resurrection came the glory of the ascension. By submitting to death, Jesus pioneered the way for the rest of humanity to enter into the eternal realm. Other people had died and been resurrected – half a dozen, I think, recorded in the Old and New Testaments up to that point plus a couple of others who came later in the period of the Acts of the Apostles – but, of course, they subsequently died like the rest of us. On the other hand, Enoch and Elijah and possibly Moses had been assumed or translated into heaven without dying. However, Jesus is unique in having passed through all three transitions. He died, then he was resurrected and finally he was translated into heaven. Jesus thereby pioneered the way for humanity to reach the eternal realm of the Father: dying, rising and ascending.

> *Therefore God also has highly exalted him and given him the name which is above every name, that at the name of Jesus every knee should bow, of those in heaven, and of those on earth, and of those under the earth, and that every tongue should confess that Jesus Christ is Lord, to the glory of God the Father.*[16]

The end of the matter is the glory of God and in that glory we humans will find a joy that is reward enough. So let us recognize that for each of us God has a plan and a purpose. Our lives mean something and there is a personal goal for our time here on earth. We must first deal with sin under the conviction of the Holy Spirit. Then we must seek the kingdom of God and his righteousness. And then we must run with patience the race that is set before us, looking to Jesus, the author and finisher of our faith, who for the joy that was set before him endured the cross, despised the shame, and is now seated at the right hand of the throne of God.

Can we really make a difference to the world? Can we significantly influence the flow of events as the multi-faceted history of humanity unfolds? I believe we can. Because of the death, resurrection and glorification of Jesus Christ there is now the potential for the Holy Spirit of God to indwell every member of our race. To that subject we will turn in the next chapter.

Chapter 6

Spiritual Warfare

I will never forget being baptized in the Holy Spirit. In the first term of my second year at university, a freshman, who had already experienced the fullness of the Holy Spirit, enthusiastically introduced me to the subject. In 1962 evangelical Christians tended to be somewhat wary of pentecostals and charismatics and I, an ardent evangelical, was going to need a lot of persuasion to get involved in such weirdness. After many interesting discussions that year I decided to spend time during the next summer vacation studying the scriptural record of the Holy Spirit. By the time I returned to college in the autumn I was convinced that the experience was still on the agenda for Christians in the twentieth century and that, obviously, included me.

After several weeks of earnestly seeking the Lord, I was praying one evening in a student house with a number of friends when the Spirit fell upon us. It was like something out of the Acts of the Apostles. People were dropping to the floor and for several minutes I was quadriplegic, a somewhat scary experience. Then, when my muscles started to function again, I became completely "drunk". As a lifelong virtual teetotaler that is the only occasion in my life when I have experienced what I imagine to be the symptoms of being comprehensively inebriated. It was a gloriously joyful experience and no hangover the next morning either! Then the tongues began and they have been flowing ever since. Speaking in other tongues continues as a powerful weapon in my spiritual armory. When my understanding runs out and I know not how to pray I can allow the Spirit to take over, making intercession for me with the languages of men and angels.

As I look back I can now see that this experience triggered the start of a significant change in my life. I had known the Lord for over ten years and I had been baptized in water in my late teens, but I cannot recall having had before that evening the consistent sense of an invisible friend that I now take for granted. Since then I have rarely felt completely alone even when far from other people. At the time of my baptism in the Spirit the awareness of God that I had experienced sporadically since my conversion started to become more persistent and engaging. That sensation has grown over the years as I have come increasingly to enjoy my Father's presence and live as his little child. And also, God Moments have become an increasingly significant part of my story.

God Moments

A God Moment for me usually contains four elements; an arresting event causing a gut reaction that stimulates a mental process demanding a personal response. It is the unexpected coming together of thoughts, feelings, objects and events, usually as an extension of previously established patterns of experience, to produce an emphatic and novel insight that is more than the sum of the individual stimuli. It feels like being gripped by God – body, soul and spirit. It is usually something that is relevant to my particular circumstances at the time and in a handful of cases a God Moment has totally changed the direction of my life.

I think Jesus had many, seriously big, God Moments. And I think the biblical writers had God Moments. They reflected on them and verbalized them. They became convinced that they had touched on something profound and important and recorded it. Let me give you an example or two of biblical God Moments.

Isaiah, the masterful Old Testament prophet, foresaw a time in the future when the earth would be filled with the knowledge of God. There would be no more pain or death in the world. He wrote:

> *The wolf also shall dwell with the lamb, the leopard shall lie down with the young goat, the calf and the young lion and the fatling together, and a little child shall lead them.*[1]

What prompted these thoughts? What kick-started Isaiah into reflecting on these things? Well, I think he must have actually seen a wolf and a lamb or a lion and a fatling together. I am confident because I have also witnessed such an event.

On 4th February, 2007 I was watching a wildlife program on TV. Incredibly the film crew had managed to record a lioness caring for a young orphaned antelope. It was an amazing situation. You could almost see the bewilderment on the lion's face as she mothered an animal she should have been killing and eating; and indeed she was starving, because looking after her adopted baby was preventing her from hunting. The presenter actually commented that it was a biblical situation; that something must have just flipped in the lion's brain. "How many other strange things", she rhetorically asked, "are going on out there when we are not around to observe them?"

Having seen that TV program I can readily imagine that Isaiah had witnessed something similar. Then he meditated upon it. What he had actually observed could one day happen universally, and his thoughts on a future world of peace and righteousness were developed and recorded. You never know, we might be only one collective brain flip away from heaven! [2]

My second example comes from the prophet Jeremiah who records a number of these God Moments, sensory experiences that became the basis of prophetic insights. The first of these conversations with God went like this:

> *Jeremiah what seest thou? I see a rod of an almond tree. Thou hast well seen: for I will hasten my word to perform it.* (AV translation)[3]

What on earth is going on here? You need to be a Hebrew scholar or, like me, possess an analytical concordance and be prepared to do a bit of research. What you will turn up is a delightful pun. The word for almond tree is *shaqed* and the word for hasten is *shaqad*. What a wonderful sense of fun our Father has!

So that is how God Moments work. Seen from one perspective the Bible is the accumulated record of forty or so persons' God Moments over 1600 years. The same Holy Spirit who inspired those authors will guide and animate me as I read their words and the more time I spend with God the better I will become at distinguishing his voice from the other sounds in my head.

Temptation

Now I am not suggesting that my or anyone else's baptism in the Spirit is anything more than just a faint reflection of what happened to Jesus. Here was a man already in touch with God to a depth not known by any other human, before or since. He had completed an apprenticeship of learning to live in harmony with the will of his heavenly Father. He had a strong belief based on both intuition and prophecy that in some way he was destined to rule the world. He was to establish a kingdom that would have no end.

Then, following his baptism in the River Jordan, he experienced a comprehensive merger between his spirit and the Spirit of God. The Father declared him to be his beloved Son. He must have felt as if he could fly! In fact he probably could have flown. He could have raised an army and kicked the Romans out of Israel as a prelude to world domination. And in fact that is exactly what he was tempted to do in the days that followed.

The Spirit led (Mark says "immediately drove") him into the wilderness to fast for forty days and forty nights. The wilderness was probably the only safe place for him with the thoughts that were going through his mind. There he wrestled with the possibilities for exercising the immense power that was surging within him. He could end his fast by making bread from stones as a prelude to solving the world's food shortage problems. He could demonstrate his power to a flabbergasted multitude by going up onto the highest point of the temple roof and leaping off to float harmlessly down to the ground. In fact, he could take over all the nations of the world. However, drawing on his knowledge of the Old Testament, he was able to repel each of these temptations.

There have been times in my life when a season of heightened spiritual experience has been followed either by my hatching up some great new project that subsequently turned out to have been a bad idea or, much worse, being completely overcome by some lethal temptation straight from the bottomless pit. It is important for us to learn how to remain close to God while handling the power of God. Jesus perfected the art of not being blown away when God acted through his humanity and one of his most important objectives in teaching us about the kingdom of heaven is to impart that wisdom to us.

This is why the character-building process we started to look at in the previous chapter is so important. Sin must be dealt with so we can concentrate, with the convicting help of the Holy Spirit, on right living. If we are ever to be those who can act as channels for the authority and power of God then we must be secure in our daily walk with the Father. We must be repenting moment by moment of any and all events in our inner or outward life that could tarnish or corrode the shining armor of God with which we are clad and with which we must battle against the evil that is in this world.

The Finger of God

We need this spiritual armor if we are to engage in spiritual warfare. As Paul tells us, in Ephesians chapter six, we wrestle not against flesh and blood but against spiritual hosts of wickedness. He then goes on to describe the armor piece by piece.[4] We must be wearing the girdle of truth around our waist and the breastplate of righteousness. Our feet must be shod with the gospel of peace and the shield of faith carried on our arm or across our shoulders for rapid deployment against incoming missiles. The helmet of salvation must be on our head and the sword of the Spirit, the living word of God, in its sheath at our side and ready for instant action.

Take a closer look at Paul's six pieces of armor. Three of them are key components of Mary's story: peace, faith and salvation. Jesus told her, "Your faith has saved you. Go in peace." The fourth component, righteousness, was the theme we unpacked in the previous chapter. To make up the full set there are two other pieces of armor: the sword of the Spirit, which is the word of God and the girdle of truth around our waist from which the sword hangs in its scabbard. The sword speaks of the immediate, cutting edge, contextually relevant, prophetic word from God, perhaps the result of a God Moment. The girdle of truth reminds us of the Scriptures. Between these two, a sound knowledge of the Bible and a sensitivity to the Spirit of God, we can be equipped to know and to speak and to act on the divinely inspired truth in any given situation.

Now although it was Paul who developed the picture of an armed soldier to illustrate the idea of spiritual warfare it was Jesus who originated it:

> *If I cast out demons with the finger of God, surely the kingdom of God has come upon you. When a strong man, fully armed, guards his own palace, his goods are in peace. But when a stronger than he comes upon him and overcomes him, he takes from him all his armor in which he trusted, and divides his spoils.*[5]

This passage is from Luke and there are parallels in Matthew and Mark. The one in Matthew is particularly interesting because a careful comparison with Luke's words makes clear that the "finger of God" is in fact the Holy Spirit:

But if I cast out demons by the Spirit of God, surely the kingdom of God has come upon you.[6]

So in addition to his (her?) ministry as the one who convicts of sin, righteousness and judgment the Holy Spirit is the one who casts out the demons. But how, in the twenty-first century, are we to understand demons and, of course, angels?

Angels and Demons

Many people, including some Christians, dismiss angels and demons because science has uncovered explanations for phenomena that in former times were put down to the supernatural. However, the angels and the demons, according to the Bible, are created beings. They exist inside our reality system. That means they, or their activities must in principle be detectable by normal scientific investigation, even if we haven't yet been able to do so.

I find it helpful to visualize angels and demons as operating in our world at both ends of the range of size in which we humans, on a logarithmic scale, sit roughly in the middle. At one extreme they are at work in the realm of the exceedingly small, in the mysterious quantum activity that generates our world "from the bottom up". At the other extreme they work on the enormously large, tweaking the complex patterns and networks of terrestrial and cosmic objects and energies and thereby guiding the course of events "from the top down". In both cases it would be difficult for us to detect their activity because our position in the middle of that spectrum of size gives us a very different perspective on the universe.

It seems to me that the angels form a proactive connection between the eternal realm of God and the temporal realm of the creation. This arrangement is necessary for two reasons: an imperfect creation cannot tolerate direct contact with God's perfection; and God cannot play a direct role in the created order (just as Shakespeare cannot be inside one of his own plays).

So the angels are responsible for executing the thinking and intentions of God within the creation and providing a local response on behalf of God to the stream of events. Those events, of course, include our prayers, but more of that later. They are organized as God's army – remember Gethsemane's twelve legions – an extension of God himself. They are able to subtly influence the way things unfold without, for the most part, our being aware of their presence. On occasion, though, they might directly activate our neurons and appear visibly and tangibly to us, seemingly physical but without the need for actual materialization.

In this model of angelic life the demons would be a rogue subgroup of angels who have rebelled and become detached from God's army, taking up permanent residence inside the creation and forming their own independent network. There is a war being fought between these powers of good and evil at both the top (very large) and bottom (very small) levels of physical reality. Whether consciously or not we humans are caught up in this war and the gospel of the kingdom is ultimately about us developing the power to advance the good and defeat the evil as we collaborate with the indwelling Spirit of God. I find this visual scheme helpful but feel free to develop your own if it does not work for you.

Sanfilippo Syndrome

What is certain is that Jesus believed in the devil and his servants. As we have seen he said that his power over demons was evidence of the kingdom of God. Was he just using the vocabulary and ideas of the time because if he had explained to his listeners that the bizarre behavior of someone like my nephew Daniel, for example, was the result of a lysosomal storage disease, a genetic aberration causing excessive levels of mucopolysaccharide in the cells of the central nervous system, his listeners would not have understood what he was talking about? More likely is that Jesus did not have that level of insight into the diseases he was healing; his understanding was bound by the limits of contemporary medical knowledge, as indeed is ours.

We do not know how Jesus conceived angels and demons but it was almost certainly not in terms that would be compatible with our science. That does not mean they are non-existent. It means we must look for a different descriptive model. I can see demonic activity at the root of Daniel's problem but not as a gang of imps with horns and tails living inside his body. Rather I see them as being responsible at the atomic level for creating the Sanfilippo gene defect that deprives his biochemistry of the normal recycling and purification process and thereby causes the accumulation of rubbish in his brain cells. If the historic Jesus could visit Daniel today he would probably carry out an exorcism. The fact that it would take effect in Daniel's chromosomes doesn't actually matter; the end result would be exactly the same.

Furthermore, when medical science eventually finds a cure for Sanfilippo syndrome it will be a victory for the angels and their "top-down" encouragement to our scientific researchers. Because the resultant therapy will be available to thousands of Sanfilippo sufferers and not just Daniel alone the benefit will be of far greater magnitude than just one miraculous healing. Needless to say I am praying for both of those outcomes.

I have argued earlier that Jesus in his earthly existence, from a strictly historical terrestrial standpoint, was human, completely human and nothing but human. However, whatever your Christological views there is no reason to insist that in matters of medical science Jesus knew anything more than the best knowledge of his day nor that he needed to know more in order to do the will of the Father. All that mattered was that he was in tune with God and able thereby to heal, within certain limits and provided there was not too much negativity around, any disease or disorder referred to him.

An Average Bunch of Guys

Wind the clock forward to today. Does God's power to work through us in the twenty-first century depend on our understanding the scientific basis of the problem we are trying to solve? In ten years' time the science could be totally different, today's theories having been replaced because of new discoveries. (Perhaps we will have invented a demon detection device! Shades of Ghost Busters!) Will we never be capable of healing diseases or sorting out family problems or restoring business prosperity or preventing economic meltdown or eliminating terrorism or reversing climate change or repairing any other dysfunction in our complex modern world until we understand everything? However much we know or think we know today we are still in exactly the same position as Jesus: it is not what we know but whom we know that matters.

Jesus delegated his ministry of preaching the gospel of the kingdom accompanied by healing of the sick and casting out of demons to the Twelve[7] and subsequently to seventy others.[8] After Pentecost others outside the Twelve took up the ministry.[9] Based on what I consider to be a misinterpretation of 1 Corinthians 13:10 some Christians hold the view that with the completion of the Bible this particular ministry ceased. The evidence of the past half-century suggests otherwise..

The twelve apostles were a pretty average bunch of guys. They were far from perfect. One of them, Judas Iscariot, after having spent time preaching the gospel of the kingdom, presumably with attendant miraculous signs, turned out to have a character flaw so serious that he became a traitor. Peter, destined to become the first church leader, cracked under pressure at Jesus' trial. Some of them started out not believing in the Resurrection, even with the evidence before their eyes. In fact these people were very much like you and me. (The student friend who introduced me to the Baptism in the Spirit in 1962 has since abandoned his faith and become an atheist.)

Of course, nothing can replace the apostles' unique personal experience of the historical Jesus and their witness to his death and resurrection. I take nothing away from their privileged position in this regard. However, stand back and ask yourself whether there is any scriptural or logical reason why the message with its powerful means of propagation that was delegated to Peter and the other members of that first group of people should not also be delegated to us today? It will need to be transposed into the context of the twenty-first century because demons have even more opportunity for causing havoc in our complex technological society, but the basic human needs have remained much the same.

So how do we get in tune with God? What was Jesus' secret? He had high expectations of us. He said that we could equal and even exceed the works that he did. What did Jesus teach and exemplify about attaining that goal? How far can we go in this total healing vocation? What are the limits? Does the Bible give any clues as to the timescale for the full realization of the kingdom of heaven? Luke begins his Acts of the Apostles by stating that what he had written previously in his Gospel was an account of *all that Jesus began both to do and teach.* The kingdom of heaven is to go on expanding and prospering – through human beings like you and me.

Cod's Mysterious Ways!

The subject of the kingdom of God is vast and we must expect our understanding to develop over time. This kingdom is not defined by a set of theological principles or a pile of rules for living but it is a dynamic and creative realm directed and empowered by the Holy Spirit. When the disciples asked the risen Jesus if he was about to restore the kingdom to Israel he told them, in effect, that they had asked the wrong question. It was not for them to know the times or seasons, but they would receive power when the Holy Spirit had come upon them.[10] That still holds good for us today. Our heavenly Father is not going to satisfy our curiosity with answers to all our questions in advance. He wants us to stay close to him because that is good for our relationship and, although he knows what is on the final page, he is largely making the story up as he goes along!

In the black comedy movie *Keeping Mum* the actor Rowan Atkinson, who has made a specialty over the years of portraying eccentric men of the cloth, plays the kindly but preoccupied vicar of Little Wallop, Walter Goodfellow. Walter is invited to deliver the keynote address at a convention of clergy. After some typically Atkinsonian confusion over "Cod's Mysterious Ways" he speaks on the subject of "God's Mysterious Ways". He concludes, "God is mysterious and we must just learn to live with it!" Amen to that!

Jesus told parables about the kingdom which were intended to hide the truth from most of his listeners. He did, however, drop a few hints along the way, and these may have been intended for our benefit. He indicated that there would be a progressive understanding of the meaning of his parables. He said, *whoever has to him more will be given.*[11] He also said, *every writer, instructed concerning the kingdom of heaven, is like a householder who brings out of his treasure things new and old.*[12] I think this should encourage us to anticipate new understanding of old ideas provided we approach the Scriptures with care under the guidance of the Holy Spirit.

Access to the Holy Spirit makes possible new experiences of God's love every day. God moves on continually creating and healing, often slowly, sometimes in a great burst of originality, but always moving forward. Jesus was the role model for living this way. He said that he did only those things he saw the Father doing. He went with the Divine flow. However, Jesus was a man of the Scriptures – we know that from his adolescent temple foray with the religious leaders and his wilderness confrontation with the devil – so we must also be people of the Book. To adopt Paul's metaphor we must be wearing the girdle of truth.

The Scriptures

More than twenty years ago I took a course in advanced motoring run by the Police. This included some revision of basic stuff like the Highway Code and how to handle a steering wheel and grip a gear stick, but its main value came from the practical training in things like making progress, assertive driving, acceleration sense, reading the road, appropriate speed, and so on. The written basis for this course was a book called *Roadcraft*. My instructor told me he would teach me how the Police themselves are taught so that after I had completed the course I could adapt what I had learned into my own driving style. I had already logged up half a million miles when I took the course, but he put the fun back into driving. Today he is still the voice in my head whenever I am behind the wheel.

I view the Bible somewhat like the *Roadcraft* manual and the Holy Spirit as my driving instructor sat beside me in the passenger seat. The Scriptures provide the fixed points of reference (the girdle of truth) and the Spirit guides and empowers the spontaneous freedom (the sword). The outcome is a dynamic and creative process of change. The Message translation of Paul's words to Timothy catches this feeling particularly well:

> *Every part of scripture is God-breathed and useful one way or another – showing us truth, exposing our rebellion, correcting our mistakes, training us to live God's way. Through the Word we are put together and shaped up for the tasks God has for us.*[13]

Studying the Bible is not about accumulating head knowledge of a set of creeds to be believed or rules to be slavishly applied each day. It is about training in God's gymnasium in order to gain spiritual fitness, shaping up to live life to the full. In tackling this training program the Holy Spirit is our coach, and Jesus is our role model. Our goal is to be like him. (We will be expanding this gymnasium idea in the next chapter.)

The authority we acquire thereby is not exercised in a worldly way. It does not depend on natural strength or knowledge or wisdom or financial wizardry or political power or military might or personal charm. It is forged and wielded within the intimate relationship between the foot soldier of the kingdom and his or her heavenly Father. You can see this exemplified in the life of the Master and explained in his teaching. Human wisdom is replaced by directly accessed wisdom from the throne room of heaven as we don the girdle of truth and wield the sword of the Spirit.

The Eyeball- Eating Worm

This picture of a battle for possession and control of planet Earth between the forces of evil and the forces of good goes a long way in my mind towards offering an explanation for what is generally regarded as Christianity's biggest intellectual problem, the existence, and indeed the sheer scale, of pain and suffering in our world. It seems that God must be lacking in either love or power or both if he cannot or will not do something about this situation. If God is omnipotent then could he not have created a world without pain? Since clearly he did not create a world without pain then he cannot be omnipotent, or, if he is omnipotent then he cannot be all-loving.

Yet being omnipotent does not mean God can do what is intrinsically impossible. His goal appears to have been a family of umpteen billion individually unique kids all of whom have come to accept his paternal wisdom and direction over their lives through their own volition. There is essential goodness in being free to make choices between real alternatives. Freedom is inherently better than slavery and only if we are truly free can we choose to be good. And it is only if we have the ability to choose to be good that we can be perfect in the same way that our heavenly Father is perfect.

In order for humans to have such freedom of choice it has to be built into our minds and our minds are dependent on our brains. Those brains consist of atoms. Therefore, freedom of choice has, in some sense, to be built in at the atomic level. However, the atoms of our brains are identical to the ones that make up everything else in the universe. There is nothing unique about the materials in our human bodies. We are composed of the same stuff as the dust of the ground. In the course of our lifetime our bodies are replaced, part-by-part, several times, from the dust. When we die the atoms that compose our bodies return to the dust. So freedom of choice has to be built into all the atoms that exist.

Human free will can only exist within a scheme of physical reality, a universe, which is free to explore and create new forms of existence. The inevitable consequences of setting up such a system include, for example, tectonic plate movements that cause earthquakes and tsunamis and the evolution of worms that can live only by feeding on human eyeballs. The alternative would have been a deterministic universe that was devoid of ugly bits but unable to respond to God. Jesus attained perfection through building his relationship with God amidst pain and suffering.

To speak about freedom of choice for an inanimate object such as an atom or a rock does not make any obvious sense. However, they do have unpredictability and that is a kind of freedom. One of my several mountaineering close shaves involved the breaking away of a large boulder just as I hung my weight on it. That was just one rock in Wales but in the Mattertal in Switzerland some years ago the whole side of a mountain detached itself and crashed down into the valley, diverting the course of the Matter Vispa River and necessitating the rerouting of the railway that runs up to Zermatt. I am very glad I was not clinging to a boulder on that mountain when it "decided" to go its own way.

Joy Replaces Pain

Sir David Attenborough cites the case of the eyeball-eating African worm as an example of the kind of natural phenomenon that makes it impossible for him to believe in a benign creator. However, human free will is only possible because freedom is woven into the fundamental fabric of existence, and that means nature must be free to evolve obnoxious worms. It is because he possesses free will that Sir David can pursue his fascinating studies and entertain us with his knowledge. However, nasty worms inevitably come with that free will package and tsunamis are part of an intricate ecological process without which complex forms of life like humans could not have developed.

Now let us introduce into this picture the angels and the demons. For billions of years before humans arrived on the scene the war for control of earth was being waged between the forces of good and evil. Battles at the sub-atomic level and at the cosmic level were being fought continuously between these two armies. Evil would gain a victory in corrupting a vital genetic code and a worm that feeds on eyeballs would come into existence. Then good would win a skirmish at the cosmic level and a huge meteorite would destroy the dinosaurs and pave the way for mammals to become a major player in the successive development of species.

The only thing that can decisively alter this balance of power is intervention by God himself, yet in a way that does not override the inherent freedom of the creation. So the agent for this intervention turns out to be an earthly species made in the image of God and capable of being perfect in the same way as

God is perfect through the use of its freedom of choice to choose good rather than evil. (It seems the morality of the angels is binary: they can be completely good or completely bad, but nothing in between.) Therefore, enter the human race, made a little lower than the angels, but set to rise above them and eventually rule the creation with glory and honor. And leading the charge towards that goal is Jesus, the author of our salvation who was made perfect through suffering.

It is recorded in all four Gospels, and there are not too many things that are recorded in all four Gospels, that Jesus is the one who will baptize us with the Holy Spirit. Having completed his course on earth he was exalted to the right hand of the Father from where he is pouring out the promised Holy Spirit. There is a fully paid-up member of the human race seated at the executive desk of the universe and controlling the supply of the Holy Spirit to all humanity. Now, let us be clear, the Holy Spirit is not some kind of magic potion; the Holy Spirit is the third member of the Trinity, fully God in every respect. Yet the channel through which God the Spirit enters the world, the world that God created and sustains in existence, the world that totally belongs to God, is through a human, Jesus Christ, bestowing the power and presence of Almighty God on his fellows.

Now the way is opened up for good to triumph over evil and for joy to replace pain as we, the little children of our Father, meet him through the indwelling Holy Spirit and join with him and the angels to do battle with the forces of darkness that are at work in our world.

Chapter 7

Your Kingdom Come

It was ten o'clock in the morning on Sunday, 5th January, 2009. I was thinking and writing about the Sermon on the Mount when out of the blue I felt led to break off in order to meditate on the words of the prayer that forms the very heart of the Sermon and that has come to be known as the Lord's Prayer. When I returned to my keyboard after half an hour Microsoft Windows, the operating system of the computer, advised me that an illegal operation had been performed and that the document, which has subsequently become this book, was now "read only" and could not be edited.

Being something of a digital dinosaur and having learned only recently that mouse mats came from PC World rather than Pet Planet, I was dismayed by this peevishness on the part of an inanimate machine. Thankfully it capitulated and restored normal service after some frantic and inexpert key tapping on my part.

In the meantime, though, I had formed the distinct impression that this was all intended to get my attention and that the Boss wanted a word with me. Five emotional minutes later I had become the recipient of a very strong impression along the lines of:

You are on Holy Ground so watch what you are doing.

Call me spooky or barmy if you like but how do we expect Father to get our attention in this technological world? Moses encountered God in a burning bush but environmentalism and the need for a risk assessment would probably rule that out nowadays. God used a donkey to get through to Balaam but I don't have one of those. In any case, such use of a donkey today would probably constitute an infringement of its animal rights. To me it was a strong God Moment and I recall it very clearly as I come now to develop the material for this chapter.

The disciples must have heard Jesus repeat many aspects of his teaching as he traveled from town to town talking to groups large and small. I cannot imagine that in the manner of Michelle (of the Resistance) Dubois in the classic 1980s TV serial comedy *Allo, Allo!* Jesus prefaced one unique presentation of his key ideas with the admonition, "Listen very carefully, I shall say this only once!" However, Matthew, in chapters five to seven of his Gospel, has gathered around one particular occasion on a mountain, a rich collection of Jesus' teachings about the kingdom of God.

It is an important feature of Jesus' gospel that people can be, and often are, good. I am frequently impressed and encouraged by evidence of that reservoir of goodwill that lies in the heart of most humans. However, I am just as frequently horrified by the extent to which pure evil can dominate the character and behavior of a small but highly influential minority. The kind of world that Jesus described in his Hilltop Homily can only come about if the balance between goodwill and evil is permanently shifted. It can only happen if the vast majority of humans are behaving in the manner described by Jesus, mutually reinforcing the good and freezing out the evil.

Miracle on the River Kwai

Is this merely a pipe dream? Could the world ever be like that? Well, there is evidence that in communities isolated from the mainstream of society by physical boundary or social distinction goodwill can take over as the dominant pattern of behavior. The very early history of the church shows that this can happen when social and spiritual factors define a particular group, and a more recent example of similar behavior inside an isolated community would be that which developed within a Japanese prisoner of war camp described in the book *Miracle on the River Kwai.*[1]

In both these cases the community did not survive. The church drifted off course and was eventually hijacked by the Roman Empire. The Second World War came to an end and the prisoners went home to an increasingly selfish and materialistic society. The common factor in both cases was contamination. The early church absorbed Roman methodology and the POWs became diluted through dispersion.

So, if what can happen on a small scale is ever to happen universally, the same level of reinforcing feedback that pertains to isolated communities would have to become ever-present. That could only be the case if all the transformed communities were each of them neighbor to other transformed communities. That in turn could only happen when the transformation process has already penetrated human society to an extent that the untransformed part of humanity becomes isolated and reduced to a level that renders it incapable of contaminating the transformed part.

So, I am thinking that there must be a tipping point or a critical level of goodwill beyond which benevolence becomes the norm, and if ever we succeed in reaching that threshold then Jesus' world vision will be attained and sustained. The question is how that is to be achieved. I believe the Lord's Prayer holds some important answers.[2]

Lord, Teach Us to Pray

This model prayer falls into three parts. The first part and the third part are about God, his fatherhood, his name, his kingdom, his will, his power and his glory. Every one of those nouns deserves to be written large and bold:

- **The FATHERHOOD of God**
- **The NAME of God**

- **The KINGDOM of God**
- **The WILL of God**
- **The POWER of God**
- **The GLORY of God**

These were the six things that I was moved to focus on that day when my computer turned into Balaam's donkey, my own personal Moses' bush, burning but not consumed. If at this point you were to stop reading and spend half an hour just thinking about what those words mean then perhaps you might experience that same sense of awe that overcame me.

What is the kingdom of heaven? Can we encapsulate the essence of this whole new way of understanding God's purpose in a few sentences?

- The kingdom is not a set of rules for outward behavior but internal qualities, inspired by the Holy Spirit: righteousness, love, joy, peace, patience, gentleness, kindness, faith, meekness and self-control.

- The kingdom is propagated by spiritual power rather than preaching.

- The Father transfers individual people from the power of darkness into the realm of his beloved Son where they serve him with reverence and godly fear.

- Suffering and tribulation will be experienced en route, but eventually glory, because the kingdom is unshakeable and everlasting.

- The poor are and always will be its main priority.

- Eventually all other forms of human government will be

replaced by it as humanity of its own free will, submits to the benign rule of God over individual hearts and minds.

That is a digest of the thinking of four early Christians, Peter, Paul, James and John[3] and it is wholly consistent with Jesus' teaching about the kingdom.

Heaven and Earth Coalesce

The kingdom of God will be complete when the intentions of the Creator are fully implemented throughout the entire creation. Jesus exemplified in his life, expounded in his teaching and established through his actions God's blueprint for each human. Thereby he gives us a glimpse of our destiny. The goal of history, according to John, is that the kingdoms of this world will become the kingdom of our Lord and of his Christ, the kings of the earth bringing their glory and honor into the holy city where God reigns forever.

This benign rule of God over the freely surrendered hearts and minds of all people, the establishment of a just, peaceful, prosperous and compassionate human society will complete the incarnation of God into our world. Heaven and earth will coalesce[4] and thereby fulfill the joy of both God and God's creatures. Paul expresses this thought in his letter to the church at Ephesus:

> *(God) purposed in himself, that in the dispensation of the fullness of the times he might gather together in one all things in Christ, both which are in heaven and which are on earth.*[5]

God is the ground and goal of all that is, the alpha and the omega, the beginning and the end. God cradles creation in the palms of his hands, as it develops towards his heart and mind, and we humans are leading this growth into God's inner life. God's will is to complete through us the incarnation supremely pioneered by Jesus.

When that happens God will, so to speak, have acquired a body, the new heaven and earth, and we will have become its nervous system, fully integrated with the mind of God, participating in the life of God and expressing that life throughout the cosmos. When that has come about the kingdom will have arrived and the will of God will be being done on earth as it is in heaven. The one upon whom this whole enterprise pivots is Jesus.

I picked up the idea of the human race being the nervous system of our world from Daniel Dennett. I find it a helpful way of looking at the kingdom echoing as it does Paul's idea of the Body of Christ. Of course, at present this nervous system is highly dysfunctional. Indeed there are many places in the world where "nerves" are destroying other "nerves". A huge amount remains to be done to bring about the unity and glory of humanity, and when we get into that discussion Dennett's atheistic philosophy has little to offer because there can be no purpose, no ultimate goal in his godless universe and no superhuman power to effect change.

So, to be inspired by the vision of where we are headed, we should focus on those six nouns with which the Lord's Prayer begins and ends: the fatherhood, name, kingdom, will, power and glory of God. Then we will be ready for the middle section of the prayer.

Food, Forgiveness and Fortitude

The heart of the prayer gives us vital information on how we can play our part in bringing this to pass. It contains three requests for us to make to God. We must ask him for daily bread, forgiveness and deliverance from temptation and evil. These are needs that we each have and as the Father's little children it is good to voice them to him. In the words of the Message translation:

Keep us alive with three square meals. Keep us forgiven with you and forgiving others. Keep us safe from ourselves and the Devil.

To pray those words reminds us that we are totally dependent on God for our very existence and survival. The whole universe exists because of God's ongoing creative activity and we are as much a part of that process as the stars. Bread can be seen as representing all of our physical needs, forgiveness as expressing our psychological needs and deliverance as typifying our spiritual needs.

But I think the prayer goes deeper. As we walk further along the path of discipleship the prayer reveals another aspect. It moves on from being just a set of very necessary personal requests to becoming in addition a series of prophetic insights and statements of intent. I will always be my Father's little child but I also have to learn how to play my part in the family business. With that in mind let us look at each of the three requests.

1 Give us this day our daily bread

I think Jesus had more than just material food in mind. Look at the context. Immediately before presenting the prayer he had said:

Don't keep on repeating yourself. Your Father knows the things you need before you ask him.

And a few sentences later he said:

Do not worry, saying, "What shall we eat?" ...Your heavenly Father knows that you need these things.

Against that background I think Jesus is implying something more than praying each day for food and we should, therefore, look for a metaphorical meaning. We do not need to search very far to find one. Jesus said to the tempter in the wilderness:

> *Man shall not live by bread alone but by every word that proceeds from the mouth of God.*[6]

Jesus is talking about hearing words from God. He adds the epithet "daily" in a clear reference to the manna that kept the people of Israel alive during their desert wanderings. The manna arrived fresh every morning but went putrid if left overnight. We need fresh words from our Father every day.

Every act of creation starts with a word from God.[7] To participate in that creative flow we need to be hearing from God. Prayer is not about us trying to get our agenda onto heaven's priority list. Rather it is about us discovering the mind of God and enacting it in our world. The deal is already done in the mind of God, but he has chosen to use us to bring it about. That is one heaven of a privilege and a responsibility. It also comes at a price; trouble comes with the territory:

> *Blessed are you when they revile you and persecute you, and say all kinds of evil against you falsely for my sake. Rejoice and be exceedingly glad, for great is your reward in heaven, for so they persecuted the prophets who were before you.*[8]

However, note the word "prophets". Jesus' likening of his disciples to the prophets of former times makes the important point that his followers are to perform that same prophetic role. The disciples of Jesus, following in a long and honorable tradition, must each aspire to the prophet's mantle. We have already caught several glimpses of this idea but now let us drill down into the heart of the matter.

The first mention of a prophet in the Bible is in Genesis 20:7. For at least the second time in his life, Abraham was in trouble for having married an extremely beautiful woman. Sarah must have been absolutely gorgeous; even at ninety years of age she was still pulling them in! It appears that to discourage the local kings, between whose countries the nomadic Abraham commuted, from killing him to steal his wife, Abraham would tell them she was his sister (which actually she was, fifty percent). The problem with this strategy was that the host monarch usually assumed he had a free hunting license and the addition of Sarah to his harem became top priority.

This time it was Abimelech, king of Gerar. Fortunately God stepped in and appraised Abimelech of the situation and Abimelech, who seemed to have been at heart a decent sort of chap, backed off. However, in the process an important aspect of the role of the prophet was defined. God told Abimelech that Abraham was a prophet and that Abraham would pray for him and Abraham's prayer would save him from being struck dead.

Abraham's credentials as an intercessory prayer warrior had been established some time earlier at the judgment on Sodom and Gomorrah. (See Genesis chapter eighteen.) The really interesting thing is the linking of the two ministries, prophet and intercessor. You see the whole scene played out as God decides to share his plans with Abraham and Abraham negotiates with God in an attempt to get those wicked cities off the hook. Abraham was the first prophetic intercessor.

Perhaps the most dramatic statement in the whole of Scripture on the role of the prophet is in Amos 3:7:

Surely the Lord God does nothing, unless he reveals his secret to his servants the prophets.

I get goose bumps every time I read those words. The Sovereign Lord of the universe has chosen to limit his actions in this way. He will not make a move before he has shared his plan with a human mind and he comes to us, according to Genesis 18, prepared to discuss and negotiate that plan. It seems that God needs someone on the inside; the nervous system must be functioning properly if God's purposes are to be realized.

Now move that principle back into the discussion of the Lord's Prayer. When we are burdened with the needs of a particular person or faced with a tough problem or a tricky situation we need to come to God and say, "Father, what do you reckon about this person or about that problem or about such a situation? Please give me your thoughts on this. My inclination is to speak or act in this particular way, but what do you counsel? What is your word on this matter? Please feed me with your living bread from heaven, a prophetic insight that will enable me to make a power-filled intervention and obtain the very best outcome in this case."

My Father wants to share his mind with me. I can work with him to discover the best way forward in relation to any person or situation. Sometimes this comes as a distinct word; more often it forms as a general impression that has to be verbalized in order to make it into a prophetic statement that can be shared with others. Always one must be willing to listen to the insights of other prophets and evaluate collective wisdom but ultimately we become the channel through which healing or creative change is effected. To keep that channel from getting clogged up we need to attend to the second key matter in the core of the Lord's Prayer:

2 Forgive us our debts as we forgive our debtors

Back in the 1970s, during the troubles in Northern Ireland, London became a target for IRA bombers. In one of the explosions at a major rail terminus a commuter was killed. The Daily Telegraph carried an interview with the man's widow soon after this terrible event in which she said that she had already forgiven the perpetrators. When asked why she had done this she said that her husband would have wanted it because in life he had been a very forgiving man.

The Dalai Lama has said about forgiving one's enemies:

> *It is one of the most important things. It can change your life. To reduce hatred and other destructive emotions, you must develop their opposites – compassion and kindness. If you have strong compassion, strong respect for others, then forgiveness is much easier... I use a meditation technique called giving and taking. I visualize and send my positive emotions like happiness and affection to others. I visualize receiving their sufferings, their negative emotions. I pay special attention to the Chinese, especially those doing terrible things to the Tibetans. As I meditate I breathe in all their poisons, hatred, fear, cruelty. Then I breathe out all the good things like compassion and forgiveness.*[9] (The Dalai Lama. *The Wisdom of Forgiveness)*

Forgiveness generates love, and love generates forgiveness. Forgiveness is the thin end of the wedge of love. We have seen that clearly in Mary's story. If we want to spread love around then we must be forgiving. When we do that forgiveness and love will be reciprocated. The request to God to forgive us as we forgive others develops into a desire that God will continually replenish our spiritual reservoir as we channel love and forgiveness to others.

In turning now to consider the third request in the Lord's Prayer let us bear in mind the theme we have noted in the first two requests. We are not just recipients of the grace of God we are also and most importantly the channel through which that grace is conveyed to others. We are the nerves, the fiber optic cables through which the word of God reaches, touches and changes the world. We are the conduits through which the forgiveness of God connects with and heals the human race. We are the friends who request from the Father bread to feed the hungry travelers who arrive unannounced in the middle of the night. That pattern will help us to unpack the third request.

3 Do not lead us into temptation, but deliver us from the evil one

When you think about it this is a strange thing to be asking God. Why would God lead anybody into temptation? On the other hand if he has a good reason for doing so, and I believe God always has a good reason for whatever he does, then why should we be asking him to stop doing it? Seeking an answer to these questions, I did a bit of research into the two words "lead" and "temptation". The more usual New Testament rendering of the word here translated as "lead" is "bring" or "carry" and the fundamental meaning of the Greek word translated "temptation" is "trial, test, probation or exploration". So if we change "lead" into "carry" and "temptation" into "test" we get:

Please do not carry us into the test but deliver us from the evil one.

If we now place the main emphasis on the word "carry" then we will get a fresh insight into the meaning of the sentence. We are not asking to avoid exploratory and testing experiences; rather we are saying we do not wish to be carried into them; we want to walk into them under our own steam. However, in recognition of our weakness and inexperience we are asking our Father to step in if things start to get out of hand.

In other words this is a commitment to the character building process that requires us to be exposed to testing and trial by pressure. Just as our bodies respond to physical stress by increasing in stamina and strength so also our spirits respond to spiritual stress. If we are going to be more effective as the prophetic salt and light in the world then we must give ourselves wholeheartedly to the training process that will produce that result. Without pain there is no gain.

If you have done weight training or watched others doing it

then you will be familiar with the situation where one person is performing an exercise and their partner is helping them by standing close to them and being ready to relieve some of the weight as the muscles approach the point of failure. That enables the person doing the exercise to safely push him or herself right up to the limit. It is this extreme stress on the muscle that causes it to get thicker and stronger.

In similar fashion, as we approach the point of spiritual failure Father takes just enough of the weight from us to allow us to complete the task or survive the stress or overcome whatever we are facing. Paul sums this up neatly:

> *No temptation (testing) has overtaken you except such as is common to man; but God is faithful, who will not allow you to be tempted beyond what you are able, but with the temptation will also make the way of escape, that you may be able to bear it.*[10]

So, here we are in God's gymnasium, learning to be effective agents in God's kingdom, discovering how to walk in the Spirit and to be led by the Spirit. The kingdom of heaven must first be established in our own heart and mind. We need depth of character to handle the power of God without being sucked into self-glory, material gain or spiritual pride.

Spiritual Weight Training

In the opening ten verses of Matthew chapter five we are introduced to the gym training routine that Jesus gave to those who were *"apprenticed and committed to him"*, the Beatitudes. Jesus brackets this eightfold list of spiritual weight training exercises with the phrase: *"for theirs is the kingdom of heaven."* To my mind that implies more than just being a citizen of the kingdom, a subject of the King: it implies stewardship or even ownership. This refers to people who are under authority and therefore entitled to hold and make use of authority. This is about possession of the kingdom, about being drawn into a deeper experience of God and his rule over and through us. The Message translation delivers the Beatitudes with fresh impact:

1. *You're blessed when you're at the end of your rope. With less of you there is more of God and his rule.*

My Father has never violated my free will. When I get off-track he allows me sufficient rope to get into a big enough tangle to make me realize I have a problem. Then, when I turn to him he shows me what went wrong. For example, I may have become frustrated when a situation that I know I should have control over does not work out. Then when I eventually realize what is going on Father starts talking. Typically he will show me that the problem is coming from elsewhere, for example, a wrong motive or a bad attitude or an act of disobedience in a matter totally unrelated to the disappointment that gave rise to the frustration. Fill in your own experiences of "rope-end" training.

2. *You're blessed when you feel you've lost what is most dear to you. Only then can you be embraced by the One most dear to you.*

Letting go and distancing myself from people who mean a tremendous amount to me has been one of the hardest things to do. There have been occasions when rescheduling that kind of emotional debt has taken years. Jesus said that there is no one who has left house or parents or brothers or wife or children, for the sake of the kingdom, who shall not receive many times more in this present age, and in the age to come everlasting life, but that can seem pretty remote when it comes to the crunch of faith. Does anyone recognize that one?

3. *You're blessed when you're content with just who you are – no*

more, no less. That's the moment you find yourselves proud owners of everything that can't be bought.

I used to really envy people who were comfortable inside their own skin. Not having inherited a particularly athletic physique I often felt despondent at school for my lack of prowess in sporting activities. The discovery of an aptitude for rowing at university and climbing in later years were godsends, enabling me to develop the most out of what I had been given. My inside life, although less obvious to other people, has been somewhat more of a problem. Learning how to replace my natural perfectionism with a God-inspired and tempered desire to be perfect has occupied most of my adult life. Are you still beating yourself up?

4. *You're blessed when you've worked up a good appetite for God. He's food and drink in the best meal you'll ever eat.*

This Beatitude and the following one form the middle of the list and they summarize the principles that Jesus designated as the two greatest commandments. I count it a blessing that working up an appetite for God has seldom been a problem for me. Only on those occasions when I hear him walking in the garden in the cool of the day and I have good reason to avoid "eye" contact does my hunger desert me!

5. *You're blessed when you care. At the moment of being care-full, you find yourselves cared for.*

Observing this, the second greatest commandment, has been a bit of a roller coaster ride for me. Moving on from childhood enthusiasm and sensitivity to finding an adult temperamental balance was not a straightforward process and involved something of an emotional meltdown in my early twenties. It took a while to recover from that experience and its legacy had both a good and a bad side: it developed my inner strength, but it also left me with a reluctance to empathize. I still need to make adjustments in that department. Is your caring nature in a healthy condition?

6. *You're blessed when you get your inside world – your mind and heart – put right. Then you can see God in the outside world.*

The goal is internal purity. It is comforting and challenging to remember that the author, the pioneer of our salvation was tempted with all the same things that we are, yet without failure. We are blessed when we endure, for when we have been proved we will receive the crown of life. The authority and power to be an agent of the kingdom depends upon this inner integrity, and that does not come through obeying the letter of any externally or internally imposed legalism but through following the Spirit of God.

7. *You're blessed when you can show people how to cooperate instead of compete or fight. That's when you discover who you really are, and your place in God's family.*

I enjoy football. Within and around a team of players there is usually intense competition. Even in the collaboration that makes a football club successful there is strong competition to gain and retain a place in the team, and the manager will make use of this to draw the best out of his players. Jesus' idea of cooperation is very different. It starts from the needs of the most disadvantaged and moves outwards from there. I am learning that there is no limit to what I can achieve as long as I do not care who gets the credit.

8. *You're blessed when your commitment to God provokes persecution. The persecution drives you even deeper into God's kingdom.*

The last thing Jesus warned in his team talk at the Last Supper, just before he prayed for his disciples, was that in the world we should expect tribulation. However, we should not become despondent, because he has overcome the world.

I hope that this brief personal commentary will have resonated with you and encouraged you in your own spiritual gymnasium of character construction. To summarize, as servants of God we must be:

- emptied of self
- detached from what is most dear to us
- content with who we are
- hungry for God
- caring for others
- internally well integrated
- keen on cooperation
- committed in the face of antagonism

We will receive from God: comfort, ownership of everything that cannot be bought, security, insight into God's working, a place in God's family and the authority to be agents of God's kingdom. This entire program is directed at producing prophetic intercessors and that brings us back to the subject of prayer.

Jesus commenced his teaching about prayer in the Sermon on the Mount by making the point that prayer is first and foremost private and solo. We must find a secret place to pray on our own, and our Father who sees in secret will openly answer us. This is personal. God is Father to all my brothers and sisters but as far as I am concerned in that secret place God is my own Father as if I were his only child. I have his total and undivided attention. Everything about this kingdom starts right there.

In those moments of self-awareness when I see clearly all my selfish, moody, petulant and ignorant behavior I know I am still a small child at heart and approaching my heavenly Father as a little child is the only way that makes sense. For all my education, practical experience of life and sophisticated conduct I am an infant that needs someone to inspire me, guide me, feed me, comfort me and clean up after me.

So, when I come to prayer it is quite natural for me to pour out my heart to God about all the things that are bothering me; the people who are sick or troubled; the terrible tragedies I have seen on TV; the problems at work; the things other people have asked me to pray about; my own personal needs; and so on. I also want to tell God about all the things I am happy or excited about. I am like a small child returning from school or a visit to a friend's house, dumping the entire story of the past few hours on a patient and attentive parent.

To omit this normal communication between child and parent would be wrong. I need to get things off my chest when I talk to my Father. However, to rush away as if that was all that had to be done is to miss out on the greater purpose of prayer. Prayer is not about me visiting the supermarket of heaven with my shopping trolley but about waiting on the King for his words.

I must enter the throne room of heaven and quietly wait for an audience with the King. There may or may not be actual words exchanged – often it is just about being deeply moved by the atmosphere in that place. Sometimes I receive clear impressions of something I should expect to happen or something I must do. Sometimes there is no clear message at the time but later events flow from that audience in an unexpectedly significant way. Nearly always I receive an infusion of the life of God, refreshing, empowering, correcting, reproving and loving me, like the little child who has just emptied his heart then being asked by his mum or dad to go and tidy their bedroom or to help by running an errand.

This solo prayer life is the necessary precursor to a collaborative prayer ministry. Joining with others to pray is essential to getting the job done but prayer teamwork has to be built on personal and private lives of prayer. There is no substitute for developing ones own personal relationship with the Lord. In verse seven of Matthew chapter six the personal pronouns change to plural and in the Lord's Prayer all the pronouns are plural. Our work as agents of the King depends on us binding many hearts together in a symphony of prayer but the ability to do that is based on the priority of each person's individual relationship with God. The members of an orchestra must spend many hours practicing on their own as well as rehearsing together for a performance.

Prophetic intercessors are to function as the catalyst for the consummation of the kingdom, not by persuasion but by prayer. The immense power of the Spirit of God is at our disposal to resolve intractable situations and transform incorrigible people. In this way we can collaborate with God to bring about change without limiting anyone's freedom of choice. Our intercession acts imperceptibly through the spiritual realm to bring about tangible results in the material world.

The Lord's Prayer – A Transliteration

So in the light of this analysis of the core of the Sermon on the Mount may I offer you the following transliteration of the Lord's Prayer:

> *Father in heaven, the self-existent One, please instill the perfection of your eternal domain into me, and my world. Grant me today my material needs and enough to share. Please supply me with prophetic and creative words to heal and inspire and to sway the course of events. Forgive me my failures as I seek to be compassionate and forgiving. Train me to become an effective steward of your kingdom, coaching me to explore and extend the limits of my spiritual capacity, yet always being there for me as I approach breaking point. So may your kingdom continually increase, revealing your power and bringing glory to you. Amen.*

But now I need to make yet another confession. Actually the pronouns in the Lord's Prayer are not singular but plural. I think it is all right for us to personalize the Pater Noster but we should never forget that it is primarily a corporate prayer. And that takes us to the subject of our next chapter: the church.

Chapter 8

The House of Prayer

I feel pretty sure that Christianity, as a religion as opposed to a divine-human relationship, was not God's preferred plan. Jesus announced the end of religion when he told the woman he met at the well in Sychar that religious worship, linked to location and occasion, would be replaced by true worship in spirit.[1] In the light of that statement we cannot hold Jesus responsible for the mishmash of competing dogma and denominations that we Christians have cooked up over the past two millennia as we have gone about building gazebos for God.

Jesus spoke incessantly about the kingdom of God but sometime in the early part of the third year of his ministry he introduced a different idea, that of church, to his disciples. Somewhere in the region of Caesarea Philippi he asked them a question. "Who do men say that I, the Son of Man am?" They mentioned various theories they had heard: John the Baptist, Elijah, Jeremiah, or another of the prophets. Jesus then asked them, "But who do you say that I am?" and it was Peter who came out with the thought that must have been forming in the back of all of their minds after two years on the road with this incredible person: "You are the Christ, the Son of the living God." After emphasizing that such an insight could only have come to Peter by divine revelation, Jesus went on to say:

> *You are Peter, and on this rock I will build my church, and the gates of Hades shall not prevail against it.*[2]

In my time as a Christian I have belonged to eight different local churches and worked with many others. In almost every case I have enjoyed seamlessly happy and fruitful times of worship, teaching and friendship and had many opportunities to serve the communities within and around those churches.

My faith roots are in the Plymouth Brethren and my childhood spiritual awakening took place in a Gospel Hall. I have fellowshipped with Baptists, Anglicans, Pentecostals and Catholics and had numerous spiritual homes because of job relocations over the decades. Latterly I experienced a geographically more settled period and membership of one of the many new charismatic churches that were spawned by the widespread renewal that took place in the final quarter of the twentieth century.

My expectation of church life grew with my years and knowledge of God. However, my experience increasingly fell short of matching it. This produced an uneasiness of spirit that I found difficult to ignore. Increasingly I found myself asking the question, "What is church?"

Then one day it came to me that I had been reversing the Master's plan. Jesus said, "go and make disciples… I will build my church", whereas I was in effect saying to him, "Lord, you make the disciples and I will build the church." I do not think I have been alone in making that mistake and the results are not good.

Relationships Versus Organization

If I had to select one reason for why the church has not turned out the way that Jesus intended then it would be that instead of focusing on relationships we have slipped into organization. And that does not just apply to the established denominations. The congregational worship and social activity of even the most unstructured protestant dissenters eventually settles into an informal kind of ritual and all such groups develop their own particular creedal and behavioral norms. A church that is initially founded on the basis of friendship can soon come to regard size as important and acquire a dedicated building closely followed by professional leadership, an authority structure and a bank balance.

Although I have spent most of my time as a Christian in the Protestant-Evangelical-Charismatic wing of the church I have made friends in many other departments. I have come to appreciate that there are good things to be found in all the different streams of Christianity. It was, for example, through Roman Catholic friends that I came to understand social action as a gospel priority flowing from and empowered by our worship and adoration of God.

Moreover, in my travels around the world I have met folk of other faiths who demonstrate personal qualities that I value as a Christian, even though their core beliefs are very different from mine. I recall an inspiring conversation with a fellow businessman in Tehran nearly forty years ago. As he shared with me his personal experience of God it came to me with some force that true spirituality and godliness can sit within and overflow Islam or Christianity or any other religious system.

Of course, the churches are generally good at meeting spiritual, practical and social needs and I would encourage any Christian, particularly a novice, to develop friendships with other believers by joining a thriving church. There are many that maintain a proper level of expectation and are healthily inclusive, avoiding delusions of grandeur, controlling tendencies and material ambitions. But are "the churches" the same thing as "the church"?

What I would like to do is explore what Jesus meant by "his church". He did not say a great deal about this subject. In fact there is so little in the Gospels compared to the rest of the New Testament that Geza Vermes concludes:

> *There is no evidence to support the idea that the foundation of the church was among the major concerns of Jesus.*[3] (Geza Vermes. *The Authentic Gospel of Jesus)*

I think Vermes is wrong. It is indeed the case that the Gospels contain just three uses of the word *ekklesia,* the word translated as church. They are found in Matthew 16:18 and 18:17. However, these two passages are crammed with information about Jesus' ideas on this subject and taken together with other scriptural evidence we can build up a picture of Jesus' vision for his church.

I Will Build My Church

We can infer that Jesus followed his father into becoming a carpenter. He would have made tables and cupboards and yokes for oxen but much of his time would have been spent on construction work. He would have cut down trees and built the scaffolding on which the masons stood to lay the stones and he would also have supplied and fitted doors, beams, flooring and other wooden items. (I picture him carrying a beam the day he told the amusing story about the plank in the eye, although if he was up a mountain at the time I guess that doesn't quite work.) Jesus was a joiner-builder, so the seven occasions in the Gospels when he used the word *oikodomeo* (build) are likely to be of interest. Let's take a look.

First there was the parable of the wise man that built his house on a rock and the foolish man that built his house on the sand.[4]

Then there was the parable of the wicked vinedressers. The landowner planted a vineyard, hedged it, installed a vat and built a tower.[5]

On another occasion Jesus criticized the Pharisees for their building of tombs for the prophets that their predecessors had murdered.[6]

Then there was the rich but foolish man who demolished his barns to build larger ones.[7] And then came Jesus' teaching about counting the cost of discipleship, which he compared to the building of a tower.[8]

On the sixth occasion Jesus was speaking about the end times, which he compared to the days of Lot when people were eating, drinking, buying, selling, planting and building.[9]

[There was one other occasion when Jesus was quoted as using, but actually and most significantly did not use, this word. At his trial he was accused of saying that he was able to destroy the temple and rebuild it (*oikodomeo*) in three days.[10] However, according to John what Jesus actually said was:

Destroy this temple, and in three days I will raise it up.[11]

The word Jesus used was egeiro, exactly the same word he used when he commissioned the disciples to go out and preach the kingdom and raise the dead (Matthew 10:8) and, of course, he was using the temple as a metaphor to represent his own body. His accusers were putting a word into his mouth that as a builder he might have used, but actually did not.]

Every one of the above six times Jesus used the word *oikodomeo* he was referring to the action of constructing a building. He never used the word loosely as we do today when we "build someone up" by praising them or "build up our hopes" or speak about "building an empire". That makes the seventh occasion, when Jesus used it of the church, particularly significant. He was introducing us to the idea of:

A Spiritual House

You are Peter, and on this rock I will build my church, and the gates of Hades shall not prevail against it.[12]

I would submit that when a professional builder who had only ever used the word "build" to describe the process of constructing houses, wine vats, towers and tombs told Peter that he would build his church and, furthermore, that he would build it on a rock, then the mental picture he had of that church was a building. There was no literal rock and Jesus did not construct a physical church building, so for just this one time he was using the word *oikodomeo* in a metaphorical sense. However, Jesus' intellectual model for his church was a building, an edifice of wood and stones, and he obviously managed to communicate this mental picture to Peter because years later Peter wrote in his first letter:

> *Coming to him as to a living stone, rejected indeed by men but chosen by God and precious, you also as living stones, are being built up as a spiritual house, a holy priesthood, to offer up spiritual sacrifices acceptable to God through Jesus Christ… The stone which the builders rejected has become the chief cornerstone.*[13]

For me this could not be clearer. We are the stones. We come to be fettled and built into a spiritual house. In repentance the untidy bits of us that will hinder the construction of a strong and well-integrated wall are chipped away. Every trace of disobedience to the Spirit of God that will limit our effectiveness is dealt with. The purpose is that as living stones, joined into one structure with Jesus the chief cornerstone, we should offer up prayers, the spiritual equivalent of the sacrifices offered up by the priests in the temple. With this in mind turn to the accounts of Jesus' second cleansing of the Jerusalem temple and feel the significance of his quotation from Isaiah 56:7:

> *For my house shall be called a house of prayer for all nations.*[14]

The purpose of the church is to intercede on behalf of the peoples of the earth. Jesus is constructing a spiritual building, founded on him as the chief cornerstone, to be a house of prayer. This is our primary activity as disciples of Jesus. Prayer is not a ritual that we follow, just one small part of our religion, one among many items on the ecclesiastical agenda; it is the primary reason for the existence of the church. Everything else on the agenda is secondary. Yes, secondary. And if a particular church has only that one item on its agenda then that is fine. In fact it is more than fine; it is to be positively commended. Because according to Jesus the only intended, the only planned activity for his church, as opposed to our churches, is to pray for the nations.

The Keys of the Kingdom

As the spiritual descendants of Abraham, Christians are destined to be the means whereby the blessing of God is imparted to the nations of the world. Jesus makes this perfectly clear when he follows up his statement of intent to build his church with the words:

> *And I will give you the keys of the kingdom of heaven, and whatever you bind on earth will be bound in heaven, and whatever you loose on earth will be loosed in heaven.*[15]

Jesus has given us the keys of the kingdom, the power to unlock the windows of heaven so that, as the Lord's Prayer says, the will of God may be done on earth as it is already done in heaven. Every single believer has that power to some extent but our full potential can only be realized when we get together. As already noted, I interpreted the Lord's Prayer in the previous chapter on an individual basis but the pronouns in that prayer are actually all plural. The word "us" dominates the Prayer.

On a visit to Nepal some years ago I watched a gang of men, in a village high in the Himalayas, building a house. As far as I could see no mortar was being used. The pile of stones ready for use had been roughly sized and sorted in the quarry, but then each one was being individually fettled on site with hammer and chisel until it fitted exactly to the stones upon which and against which it was to rest, every bump and hollow in the stone's surface matching perfectly those of its neighbors. Using this drystone building technique a house of two stories was being constructed. The friction and stability generated between interlocking stones with identical surface contours did away with the need for an adhesive substance between them.

As a construction worker, Jesus would have had ample opportunity to observe stonemasons at work. He would have had time to think about the way in which separate pieces of rock can be placed so that they interlock with each other to form a strong wall. He would have studied the way in which stones are added in overlapping layers using friction to form enduring bonds between them. On the basis of these observations it would have been perfectly natural for him to develop his ideas about the structure of the church and put them into practice in the way he organized his followers around him.

The Smith Sisters

Now let us have a bit of fun. Here is a hands-on experiment for you to try. You will need to obtain some house bricks or children's building blocks or some other block shaped objects, all of the same size. Then you will need to play around with them as I have done (see Appendix 6). If you do this then I reckon you will discover the following:

1. The largest number of bricks that can all touch each other, face to face, is four.

2. The largest number of bricks that can surround one central brick and all touch it face-to-face is twelve.

This pattern of organization is apparent in Jesus' core team of disciples. He selected twelve that they might be with him and that he might send them out to preach. Three of this group, Peter, James and John, were chosen to accompany him on special occasions that involved miraculous power, revelatory experience and strong intercession. These three were the only ones present with Jesus at the raising of Jairus' daughter, the transfiguration on the mountain and the agony in Gethsemane.

I believe that there are some important clues here for the structure and function of the church. Jesus is showing us how church is to be organized. Twelve is a good number for an effective training and working unit, and two or three plus Christ is the optimum for the most intimate fellowship enabling an intense vision, extreme prayer and the release of spiritual power. As a modern example of this at work the widespread spiritual awakening that happened in the Hebrides, a group of islands off the west coast of Scotland in the 1950s has been traced back to two elderly sisters, Peggy and Christine Smith, praying together for a divine outpouring.

In Matthew 18:15-20 Jesus develops these ideas. He first lays down a four-step conflict resolution process for dealing with a dispute between two of the brotherhood (which includes the sisterhood in Jesus' thinking!) The first step is to speak to the other person alone; if that fails then talk again with one or two others present. This highlights the inner core group of two or three. If that fails then tell it to the church, the group of twelve. Finally, if even that does not get the required result, then the offending person is to be regarded as a heathen and a tax collector.

Now Jesus had a soft spot for tax collectors, something that his critics used against him (Luke 7:34). It is, therefore, clear that Jesus is not saying that the church should cease befriending the recalcitrant brother or sister. What he is saying is that they must not, as long as the issue remains unresolved, participate in the work of the church. Jesus then goes on to define this work:

> *Whatever you bind on earth will be bound in heaven, and whatever you loose on earth will be loosed in heaven.*

Buildings, Bishops and Budgets

Where two or three gather in Christ's name he will be present spiritually with them. That group can heal and animate their environment. This gives us important information about the structure of the church. If Christ himself is present with power to save, heal and restore whenever a group of two or three people is convened in his name, what more authority is needed? If around that powerful prayer cell are gathered nine or ten other disciples at varying stages of training and development, what more is necessary to multiply and extend the work of Christ on earth?

> *Do not fear, little flock, for it is your Father's good pleasure to give you the kingdom.*[16]

The practical consequences are far reaching. No buildings other than houses are needed for meetings; no professional leadership is required; and little or no money is necessary. Buildings define boundaries and limit growth, change and movement; professional leadership engenders vested interests; and money, instead of being used to address the real needs of people, gets diverted into maintaining unnecessary buildings and paying unwarranted salaries. A church functioning according to the Jesus model would not require buildings, bishops or budgets.

We have in recent years been given a painful lesson in how destruction, suffering and death can be inflicted by guerrilla armies operating through an invisible micro-cellular organization. A similarly structured, but in every other respect diametrically opposed network of God-fearing, Christ-centered and Spirit-filled prayer warriors will be able to combat evil and administer an alternative healing and creative regime in human affairs that is imperceptible and non-coercive. This is prophetic intercession at work.

The purpose God has for his people, according to the Lord's

Prayer, is to see the will of God done on earth as it is already done in heaven. In Matthew chapters sixteen and eighteen Jesus says, first to Peter and then to all the twelve, literally translated from the Greek:

> *Whatever things you bind on the earth shall be having been bound in heaven, and whatever things you loose on the earth shall be having been loosed in heaven.*[17]

Note the careful choice of tenses. To bind and loose on earth we must echo what has already taken place in the mind of God. Prayer must be about unveiling and affirming what God has already planned in the unseen realm. It may start with asking God to intervene and change something bothering us in the here and now but it cannot stop there. Intercessory prayer goes much further.

Prophetic Intercessors

The basis for effective prayer is defined in Matthew 18:19. I cannot find a single translation to support what I am about to say which means either that I have come up with an original thought or that I am seriously off target. I will leave you to judge. It is important to note that the primitive Greek text was written without punctuation marks, so what Matthew 18:19 literally says, without any commas, is:

> *Again truly I say to you that if two agree of you on the earth concerning everything whatever they ask it shall be to them from the Father of me in heavens.*

Every one of the translations in my library places the comma after the word "ask". That causes the sentence to mean that we should be agreed about the request that we are going to make to God. However, try placing the comma after the word "everything".

The goalposts move, don't they? Suddenly it becomes a whole lot more than just agreeing what to pray for; it requires us to agree about everything. That has massive implications for the degree of transparency, meekness, compatibility, love and trust needed between partners in prayer and shows why Jesus started this passage of teaching by explaining what to do when relationships are in danger of breaking down.

Now I do not think it means we all have to agree about whether red wine is better than white (or no wine at all!) or whether left is preferable to right in politics or how old the Earth is or whether Calvin or Arminius (or both of them!) were wrong. It is not about agreement on matters that are spiritually unimportant; it is about something deeper than that. So let me take you further into the text.

The word translated "agree" is based on the Greek word for music; our English word "symphony" comes from it. English does not have the equivalent verb but we can invent it. That will cause the sentence to read:

> *If two of you down here on the earth symphonize about everything, then whatever you ask shall be done for you by my Father in heaven.*

A symphony orchestra has many different kinds of instruments, playing different tunes with different rhythm patterns, all blending together to produce a complex and beautiful sound. A clarinet is not a cello even though they are both made of wood; nor is a cymbal the same as a cornet, even though they are both made of brass. An orchestral score takes the different properties of each of the instruments and blends them intricately together.

I believe that the mission of the church, the network of friendship and prayer that unites Jesus and his followers, is to see the will of God done on earth as it is in heaven. In order to do that we will have to experience a measure of symphonic togetherness that goes much further than we might have previously anticipated. We will need to symphonize concerning everything. We will need to learn how to hear the music that is coming from heaven and harmonize our individual instruments together with that music and with each other. In terms of the stonework picture of the church our bumps and hollows must all match.

The Johannesburg Symphony

The thought that music lies at the heart of reality and that if physicists and cosmologists ever do come up with a "theory of everything" it will have to be expressed in musical rather than mathematical terms, had occurred to me some time before I came across a fascinating book by the late Arthur Peacocke, a world-class scientist, and Ann Pederson, a skilled musician, entitled *The Music of Creation.* They wrote:

> *At the heart of the music of creation is the ongoing creativity of God and God's partners. Our calling in life is to create, to improvise on the themes of God's musical works. Learning how to improvise is practicing the music of the Christian faith. Like the beat and rhythm of music, God's movement is in, with, and under us.*[18] (Arthur Peacocke and Ann Pederson. *The Music of Creation)*

Almost forty years ago I made a business trip to South Africa. I enjoyed a refreshing sleep through the night from London to Johannesburg and I had a while to wait for an onward flight to Port Elizabeth. As I walked around in the terminal building I experienced something strangely wonderful. I was "hearing" an orchestra and a choir. It had an unearthly quality in the way the notes were rising and falling in pitch and volume with different musicians and singers entering and leaving the symphony. At one point I would be in the audience, but then I would find myself in the choir or playing an instrument. There were moments when I even felt like the conductor. This went on for several minutes and when it finally faded I felt lifted and invigorated.

I had never encountered anything like that before. The experience in its fullness and intensity has not, so far, been repeated but I have been finding in recent days an increasing ability to recapture brief snatches of it. That trip to South Africa was also memorable because it marked one of the few occasions in my life when I have spontaneously offered to pray for someone's healing (Glaucoma, actually) and got a result. In my mind the music and the healing prayer were linked. I am not saying that music literally as we know it is the key to intercessory prayer but I think it may be pointing us to a deeper reality, and music is the thing closest in our experience to that reality.

Church and Kingdom

All of this leaves me hungering for an experience of church that I have yet to find. I long to be part of a symphonizing and powerful cell of two or three, that cell being part of a larger learning and working group of a dozen or so. Maybe I am being hopelessly idealistic but the thought that Jesus had something in mind for his church that I have not yet come across refuses to go away. And, of course, what I am visualizing somewhat challenges the way that corporate Christianity has developed over the past twenty centuries. It would be ludicrously presumptuous to suggest we got it entirely wrong but we do appear to have drifted off course. Geza Vermes has a pertinent comment on how this came about:

> *The New Testament concept of the establishment of the kingdom of God can neatly be divided into three phases. In the first, the kingdom was expected to be realized during the Palestinian ministry of Jesus. In the second phase, the arrival of the kingdom was to succeed the Parousia, which was expected to follow soon after the cross. In the third, the feverish waiting progressively quietened*

> *down, the date of the Second Coming was adjourned sine die, and the notion of the kingdom metamorphosed into that of the church.*[19] (Geza Vermes. *The Authentic Gospel of Jesus*)

The remaining chapters will address the manner and timing of the development of the kingdom. For now it is Vermes' last statement that I want to highlight; Christians came to confuse the kingdom with the church. However, Jesus was very clear on this point. The passage that distinguishes and connects the two concepts, church and kingdom, is Matthew 16:18, 19:

> *I will build my church, and the gates of Hades will not prevail against it. I will give you the keys of the kingdom of heaven.*

Keys are used to lock and unlock doors and gates, thereby preventing access (binding) or permitting access (loosing) in and out of a building or enclosed space. These keys were not just given to Peter personally. In Matthew 16:19 the personal pronoun "you" is indeed singular and relates to Peter as an individual. However, in Matthew 18:18 Jesus reaffirms the delegation of power to bind and loose and the personal pronoun "you" is plural. This is an example of the misunderstanding that can arise because modern English has lost this distinction between singular and plural. If you read the Authorized Version the older forms of "thee" (singular) and "ye" (plural) are evident. Therefore, the keys with the power to bind and loose that were given to Peter must also have been given to other disciples.

I have already made the point that the apostles were not special people. If the Jesus story was being played out in the early years of the twenty-first century then people just like you and I would be chosen to accompany Jesus. Most of us would turn out like Peter, James and John, and one or two might turn out like Judas Iscariot. The ministry of "binding and loosing" did not stop with Peter or the rest of the Twelve in the early years of

Christianity – just read the Acts of the Apostles – so there is no reason to restrict its scope today. Collectively we Christians are the church, the keyholders of the kingdom, but the kingdom is not the same thing as the church. The church is part of the kingdom but the kingdom is much bigger than the church.

Jesus had concentric circles of people around him. He had his closest group of Peter, James and John. Then he had the Twelve. Then there were larger groups of disciples; one hundred and twenty were present on the day of Pentecost and according to Paul five hundred witnessed a post-resurrection appearance of Jesus. Then there were the crowds that followed him or formed around him continually. On one occasion the crowd reached perhaps 10,000 or even 20,000. (5000 men plus women and children). Since the actual individuals present in these crowds would change from place to place and from week to week it is safe to assume that Jesus' actual sphere of influence was two or three times that number, perhaps 50,000 altogether.

The innermost circle would have had the most intensive and absorbing engagement with Jesus and the outermost circle would have had a much lower level of commitment or involvement. Yet all those 50,000 or so people would have been drawn into Jesus' influence to some degree and would, therefore, have come within the scope of the kingdom. The church, consisting of the innermost circles, was itself part of the kingdom but was performing the special role of keyholder for the kingdom. The church is the spiritual temple, the house of prayer that stands at the heart of the city, part of the city but exercising a distinct function within the city.

This distinction between kingdom and church has far-reaching consequences. It has the potential to provide answers to some puzzling questions. It gives new meaning to the experience of being a Christian in a secular world. It discourages the propagation of exclusive ideas that cause Christians to build unnecessary and unhelpful walls between themselves and the rest of society. It takes Christians into a new spiritual dimension, gives us a different perspective and empowers us in new ways. We will explore these ideas further in the next chapter by considering one of Jesus' seven parables of the kingdom as recorded by Matthew in chapter thirteen of his Gospel, the parable of the leaven.

Chapter 9

Leavening the Lump

I first came across yeast as a teenager when somebody gave me a ginger beer plant. This arrived in a jam jar as a pale gray-colored slurry. I had to feed it with a quantity of ginger and sugar and give it a stir each day for a week or so. Then, when mature, the slurry was tipped into a muslin bag to strain off the liquid into a large container. More sugar, lemon juice and a lot of water were added to this followed by mixing and bottling. After another couple of weeks the finished product was ready for drinking. The sediment remaining in the muslin bag could be divided into two because the yeast had multiplied during the fermentation process. At this point I could double my rate of production, give a ginger beer plant to a friend or throw one-half away.

Saccharomyces cerevisiae is a single-celled fungus. It is the biological agent that turns barley juice into beer and causes dough to rise. Each yeast cell contains all the essential components and carries out all the tasks that are performed by every cell in your body and mine. It is favored as a research model by cell biologists because it is robust and reproduces rapidly. It is a microscopic factory, a hive of activity, with protein molecules whizzing around inside so fast that they visit every part of the cell umpteen times every minute. There are departments that digest food and make energy, there are others that manufacture materials for export from the cell and there are others that recycle materials for reuse. Yet this metabolic marvel is slightly less than one-hundredth of a millimeter in diameter.

Yeast's most interesting function as far as we are concerned is to produce several enzymes, catalytic converters that work as a team to break down sugar and change it into alcohol and carbon dioxide gas. In all intoxicating beverages alcohol is the main product of interest and in beer and sparkling wine the gas also plays an important part. In bread it is the carbon dioxide gas that produces the open sponge-like texture; the alcohol is an unwanted byproduct and is driven off in the subsequent baking operation. As one who tries to avoid alcohol I have often wondered how much of it my homemade ginger beer contained!

The most prominent component of the yeast cell is the nucleus. This contains the yeast's genome, the DNA blueprint that defines what yeast is and what it does. When it comes time for the cell to multiply the nucleus replicates and this second nucleus gathers around it a share of all the other cell components prior to forming a bud that grows in size and eventually splits off as a daughter cell. This daughter goes on to maturity and then begins to reproduce. The mother cell carries on breeding daughters before dying. Actually a yeast cell does not live very long but it reproduces fast and one cell rapidly becomes two, four, eight, sixteen, thirty-two, and so on.

Bullets and Billows

Jesus selected yeast to illustrate the work and growth of the kingdom. He said that:

> *The kingdom of heaven is like leaven, which a woman took and hid in three measures of meal till it was all leavened.*[1]

In this he has given us a graphic picture of the inner structure and functioning of the kingdom. The kingdom consists of "yeast" cells that manufacture and export a spiritual catalyst that makes the people and situations around them lighter (as in bread) or happier (as in booze!) These cells also grow and produce offspring, cells of the same type that in turn go on to deliver more of the same benign influence on their surroundings. This continues until the whole of the dough is leavened. This work goes on largely in secret; the leaven is hidden in the meal and quietly gets on with its job unnoticed until the results are clear for all to see.

I would now like to place this idea of yeast alongside that of the living stones developed in chapter eight. All analogies have limitations and in order to build up a better picture of what Jesus had in mind for his church we need to draw together these two very different ideas and combine key features from each of them. Scientists are not afraid to use this technique. For example, they sometimes find it helpful to think of light as a beam of particles, like bullets shooting out of a machine gun. On other occasions it is only possible to explain the behavior of light if one thinks of it as a wave motion. These two ideas cannot be reconciled in our minds – bullets and waves are totally different things – but each of them gives important insights into the nature of light.

From the building analogy we identified the cellular structure of a dozen or so disciples gathered around a group of two or three leaders with Jesus Christ at their spiritual center. By comparing this with Jesus' strong words on the subject of the temple being a house of prayer for all nations and the promise of his presence in the middle of every group of two or three "symphonic" intercessors we came to the idea that the primary function of this cellular structured church was intercession. This was reinforced by the picture of a spiritual house composed of living stones offering up spiritual sacrifices to God that was described subsequently by Peter, the very man to whom Jesus had originally directed his words about the church.

Three Measures of Meal

In a fascinating scriptural word parallel the theme of intercession is also indicated by Jesus' choice of "three measures" as the amount of flour for the yeast to work within. Both Matthew and Luke record that Jesus specified "three measures of meal". Why? Well, it turns out that the only other reference in the Bible to "three measures of meal" is in Genesis chapter eighteen, in the passage that introduces the subject of intercession. That chapter also records what is possibly a pre-incarnation appearance of Christ as one of the three men who visited Abraham on that occasion. If so then Jesus could have had a déjà vu memory of this incident. In any event his encyclopedic knowledge of the Old Testament scriptures would have allowed this associative link to Abraham's intercession for the cities of Sodom and Gomorrah to form in his mind.

So both yeast and masonry direct our attention to the underlying theme of intercession. The stonework metaphor also nicely conveys the thought that each cell is part of a larger structure, a house of prayer, a temple. Paul latches onto this thought in his letter to the Ephesians:

> *Now, therefore, you are no longer strangers and foreigners, but fellow citizens with the saints and members of the household of God, having been built on the foundation of the apostles and prophets, Jesus Christ himself being the chief cornerstone, in whom the whole building, being joined together, grows into a holy temple in the Lord, in whom you also are being built together for a habitation of God in the Spirit.*[2]

If we now combine the picture of the building with the picture of the yeast we are able to inject substance into Peter's thought that the stones are actually alive, and like all living things they are breeding. Each yeast cell divides and multiplies giving rise to more cells. Stones give us the idea of strength and structure but we need the yeast to show us how the growth comes about.

The yeast also demonstrates, in a way that stones cannot do, the idea that the cells are having an impact on their environment. They are generating an enzyme, a chemical catalyst that beneficially changes the world in which they exist. They are continually extending this influence as they grow in numbers and penetrate every part of the flour. This activity goes unnoticed until the job is well advanced and even when it has exerted its benign influence universally the yeast always remains a relatively small part of the dough mixture.

So the ideas of the building and the yeast give us complementary pictures of the church that Jesus is constructing. Neither of these ideas is complete in isolation. Buildings do not grow by stones breeding other stones and yeast cells do not organize themselves into structures. Yet by holding both ideas in our mind and switching back and forth between them we can illustrate and gain understanding of how the church grows and how it functions.

The Tabernacle

One feature that is common to both ideas is that of the nucleus within the cell. The arrangement of stones in a wall entails sets of three or four stones all touching each other. This group forms the center of a larger group in which about a dozen stones all touch one central stone. Similarly in the yeast there is a nucleus that governs the nature and activity of the cell. This was the structure of the discipleship group around Jesus. There were twelve who were selected to be with Jesus. However, Peter, James and John formed the inner group that accompanied him when he raised Jairus' daughter, when he was transfigured on the mountaintop and when he wrestled with his greatest temptation in the garden of Gethsemane.

With this nuclear picture in mind let us focus on Jesus' idea of "a house of prayer for all nations" and Paul's description of a "holy temple in the Lord" and Peter's picture of "a spiritual house" and look at the shape of this "habitation of God in the Spirit". Several temples are mentioned and described in the Bible but the earliest and the original design is that of the Tabernacle, found in the book of Exodus.

God selected a man called Bezaleel to build the Tabernacle. Moses provided him with a general layout and a list of items of furniture and equipment and starting from these instructions the whole thing had to be designed, fabricated and constructed from a pile of raw materials. His friend Aholiab and a group of talented artisans worked with him but crucially the Spirit of God filled him with wisdom, understanding and knowledge of all the skills and techniques needed to visualize and execute the job.

I find it significant that Bezaleel is the first person in Scripture that God declares to have been filled, by God himself, with the Spirit of God. There must have been others before Bezaleel who had known the fullness of God's presence but he is the first to be specifically mentioned as being filled by God with the Spirit of God. [3] The Spirit endowed him with:

- Wisdom
- Understanding
- Knowledge and
- Workmanship

His task was to design artistic works and to execute those designs in gold, silver, bronze, gemstones, wood and textiles. The whole of human intellectual and practical creative activity is encompassed in Bezaleel's experience of the Spirit of God and the outcome was a beautiful and portable place of worship for the Israelites during the forty years spent following their own private cloud of fire and smoke around the wilderness.

Follow That Cloud

It is clear from the book of Acts that the Holy Spirit was the boss in the early church. Time and again the Spirit of God led individuals and groups into courses of action. Any model we develop for understanding the structure, growth and function of the church must be founded on the living truth of the indwelling executive presence and power of the Holy Spirit. While the church has historically acknowledged this in theory it has not consistently experienced it in practice. In my view it is only possible to know the comprehensive rule of the Spirit of God if we adopt the Jesus design for an inconspicuous cellular church that I have been unpacking in this book. From the moment we abandon that principle and introduce a visible organization of our own then decline sets in and within one generation the influence of the Holy Spirit will, for all practical purposes, have gone. The Tabernacle was demountable and portable. We must follow the cloud wherever it goes.

The Tabernacle consisted of an open-air courtyard, formed by a boundary curtain, wherein sacrifices were carried out; at the back end of this space stood a roofed tent, the Holy Place. Inside this structure were several pieces of gold furniture. Chief among these was the Ark of the Covenant, now firmly fixed in the popular mind by the cinematic exploits of Indiana Jones.

This layout resembles the structure of the living yeast cell. As with the yeast cell's outer membrane the Tabernacle had a boundary wall containing all the equipment required for the various activities to be performed. Within that enclosure was found the nucleus, the Holy Place, wherein was the Ark, the focal point for the presence of God.

The Ark of the Covenant contained the stone tablets on which were inscribed the Ten Commandments, the DNA for a God-centered and humane society. I hope by now you will be sharing my enthusiasm for the idea that the righteousness of God is not defined by a list of rules and regulations to be obeyed or a code of conduct to be followed; the life is in the Spirit of God. Yet these Ten are fundamentally important principles that we ignore at our peril. We should all make it our business to honor God, our parents and our spouse, preserve the life, reputation and possessions of others and guard our hearts from avarice. Oh, and having tried working several weeks without a break, I am convinced that one day off in seven makes a lot of sense.

If the world is ever to be transformed into the place that Jesus described in the Hilltop Homily, where humility and meekness dominate, where mercy is extended to all and peace is universal, where honesty prevails over deceit and promises are always kept, where marriage is sacred and forgiveness is universal then the Decalogue will be at the heart of it. These Ten Commandments are the spiritual equivalent of the fifteen fundamental laws of physics that define the nature of material existence. They are not by any means the whole of the story but without them no story will be possible.

Gaining Spiritual Authority – Three Steps

The outer court of the Tabernacle was open to all Jewish people but only the priests could enter the Holy Place. Offerings and sacrifices were dealt with in the outer court. If any Israelite was seeking forgiveness for some misdemeanor or had some happy event to celebrate then they were free to enter the outer court and engage with the priests in carrying out the ritual prescribed for their particular situation. However, only the priests were allowed to burn incense or tend the lampstand or replenish the shewbread inside the Holy Place. This scheme conveys the idea of closer access to God being achieved through more stringent qualifications.

Under the Old Testament law membership of the priesthood was determined by birth. Unless you were a descendant of Aaron, the original priest, then you could not be a priest. However, in Jesus' church the opportunity to become part of his inner circle is open to all. Qualifications are still needed but there are no insuperable barriers placed in the path of any genuine seeker of God. The joys, the challenges and the tribulations, the privileges, the triumphs and the costs of intercession that accompany an increasingly closer walk with the King are accessible to all.

I do not think that God places people in rigid categories and neither should we. However, to aid my thinking and understanding of Jesus' teaching I have found it helpful to visualize three levels of engagement with the kingdom of God: citizen; disciple; and intercessor. These three stages of spiritual development have emerged in several different contexts as we have considered the Gospels. We have noted the dough, the yeast and the nucleus of the yeast cell; we have thought about the city, the temple and the Holy Place within the temple; and we have observed a similar pattern in Jesus' dealings with the extended group of (120/500?) disciples, the Twelve and the inner trio of Peter, James and John.

Step One

This same pattern can also be discerned in Matthew, Luke and John's account of the Great Commission. (I am excluding Mark's heavily edited version.) Luke records Jesus' final mission statement in the following words:

> *Thus it is written, and thus it was necessary for the Christ to suffer and to rise from the dead the third day, and that repentance and remission of sins should be preached in his name to all nations, beginning at Jerusalem. And you are witnesses of these things. Behold I send the promise of my Father upon you; but tarry in the city of Jerusalem until you are endued with power from on high.*[4]

This is the most general and comprehensive version of the commission. The events of the cross and the Resurrection are stated to be the necessary grounds on which it becomes possible for sins to be remitted but in order for individual humans to appropriate for themselves a personal release from bad behavior and its consequences they must repent. This message is to be proclaimed to all nations in Christ's name. However, the benefits do not depend on the hearer intellectually assenting to the fact or the significance of the cross and the Resurrection; the active condition is repentance.

A person who is thus repenting will have become part of the three measures of meal that is being leavened by the yeast. They will have attached themselves as a traveler to the wandering nation of Israel. They will have come under the moral government of God, whether or not they believe in him. They will have taken up residence within the city walls. They will have become a citizen of the kingdom.

Step Two

Matthew's version of the Great Commission takes us to the next level, that of discipleship:

> *All authority has been given to me in heaven and on earth. Go therefore and make disciples of all the nations, baptizing them in the name of the Father and of the Son and of the Holy Spirit, teaching them to observe all things that I have commanded you; and lo, I am with you always, even to the end of the age.*[5]

According to Luke the gospel of repentance for the remission of sins is to be preached to all the nations. As a result, according to Matthew, disciples will be made of all the nations. The prepositions "to" and "of" are key words in these different but complementary versions of the Great Commission. Within every nation there will be disciples of Christ, people who have not only repented but who have gone on to be baptized in water in full acceptance of the reality of God and the unique Sonship and resurrection of Jesus Christ, who have received the gift of the Holy Spirit and God's heavenly power and who are following a pathway of obedience to all that Christ has commanded. These will have become the yeast, the Tabernacle worshippers and the living stones. They will be the light of the world and the salt of the earth. They are more than just subjects of the King; they are servants of the King and keyholders of the kingdom.

Step Three

When we come to John's version of the Great Commission we meet the third level of engagement with the kingdom, namely spiritual authority:

> *"Peace to you! As the Father has sent me, I also send you." And when he had said this, he breathed on them and said to them, "Receive the Holy Spirit. If you forgive the sins of any, they are forgiven them; if you retain the sins of any, they are retained."*[6]

Here we are getting into some really serious stuff. I cannot pretend that I fully understand what Jesus seems to be saying. I have made use of unilateral forgiveness on occasions to good effect when praying for some really intractable human situations. However, the idea of retaining somebody's sins, locking them into the consequences of their bad attitudes and actions takes some swallowing. And yet we see it happening in several case studies in the Acts of the Apostles. The deaths of Ananias and Sapphira, the denunciation of Simon the sorcerer and the blinding of Elymas are all examples of this principle in action. [7] This is an aspect of the Great Commission that we cannot ignore. The keys of the kingdom are for binding as well as loosing. The inability of the gates of hell to withstand such an onslaught implies spiritual authority and spiritual warfare.

Salvation, in the sense of being able to face Christ seated on his judgment seat with a measure of confidence that the retelling of our story in that solemn theater of justice will not be wholly embarrassing, depends on repentance. Repentance will guarantee recognition of our citizenship of the kingdom. That will be enough to ease our passage into the eternal realm. However, we can go much further in this present life. To do so requires a whole-hearted commitment to belief in the resurrection of Jesus accompanied by water baptism and the receiving of the Holy Spirit. We then become a disciple and not just a citizen, a temple worshipper and not just a subject. As a servant of the King we can play an active part in the extension of the Kingdom. We become the yeast in the dough, the living stones in the house of prayer.

The ultimate goal of discipleship is intercession, spiritual identification with the people who suffer, sharing the pain felt by the Holy Spirit and exercising the power that will bring about change in their circumstances. To be an intercessor with Jesus Christ is to travel that road with him, to experience and wield an ever-increasing measure of spiritual authority over the human and material world and to share in the sufferings of the Master.

God's Cunning Plan

The propagation of the kingdom is to be effected through the manifestation of power rather than by preaching. Paul tells us that the kingdom is not in word but in power [8] and Jesus never taught his disciples how to preach, only how to pray. The widespread absence, for many centuries, of real and tangible evidence of the Spirit of God at work in the physical world led many Christians to think that such manifestations of Divine power had died out with the Apostles and all that now mattered was the inward work of the Spirit. To a great extent the worldwide charismatic outpouring of the Holy Spirit during the second half of the twentieth century has countered that view. Unfortunately, the aberrations and excesses of an immature church, ill equipped to handle such power, are everywhere to be seen; yet such a major event must be leading somewhere. I believe God is working a "Cunning Plan".

In search of information about that plan I am going to venture into the book of Revelation. I grew up in a stream of Christianity that enthused over schemes of prophetic interpretation in which highly symbolic passages of Scripture were unpacked to reveal layers of detailed predictions about the future. I never was entirely comfortable with that approach and as I learned that human free will and the operation of chance in the world point to a God who does not determine in advance the minutiae of human history I rejected such ideas. However, one must be careful not to throw out the baby with the bath water. I have come to see that God can and does outline the future in a probabilistic way and he will patiently recycle human failure for as many times as it takes to achieve his predetermined purposes. The value of studying prophecy thus remains intact.

I was, therefore, heartened to come across a professional theologian, Alister McGrath, airing an idea derived from the book of Revelation that had been in my mind for many years. I found it in a footnote to his book *The Dawkins Delusion*. In correcting several biblical and historical misunderstandings by Richard Dawkins, McGrath makes the following observation:

> *The 144,000 are probably Christian ascetic "warriors" who are using pacifist means and spiritual warfare to resist secular atheist and cosmic evil powers.*[9]
> (Alister McGrath. *The Dawkins Delusion*)

The 144,000, referred to by Alister McGrath, appear in two passages in the book of Revelation: 7:1-8 and 14:1-5. 12,000 are drawn from each of the twelve tribes of Israel. They are called the "servants of our God", and they are sealed on their foreheads with the name of God. They are chaste, they speak without guile, and they are redeemed from humanity as "firstfruits" to God and the Lamb, whom they follow wherever he goes. They follow him to the top of Mount Zion where they are found standing without fault before the throne of God and singing a new song that only they can learn.

The 144,000 are called "the firstfruits". They are not the harvest. The main harvest follows them, an innumerable multitude from all nations, tribes, peoples and tongues that comes out of the great tribulation to serve God day and night in his temple. Despite the idea propagated by some religious sects salvation is not restricted in the Bible to 144,000 people. However, this group, symbolically numbering 144,000, does have a special role to play.

I think there is sufficient in the above description to underpin McGrath's idea of 'ascetic spiritual warriors'. In addition, though, I would suggest that this same group of people, albeit differently symbolized as "two witnesses", is also the subject of Revelation chapter eleven, where the warfare aspect appears even clearer in both prophetic power and personal suffering. After a period during which the witnesses dominate the forces of evil they are killed and their dead bodies left in the street. Then after three-and-a-half days the breath of life from God enters them and they stand on their feet to the consternation of their enemies. This echoes Jesus' prediction that the temple would be destroyed and raised again in three days.

It was an intense God Moment when I first noticed that, *"the 144,000 sang, as it were, a new song before the throne that no one else could learn"*. Shivers went down my spine as I recalled the music that I had heard in Johannesburg airport and I thought about the intimate symphonic togetherness that can empower two prayer warriors to ask anything of the Father and it will be done for them. Our goal must be to follow Christ to the top of Mount Zion where, in company with numerous others, we can join in the symphony of prayer that will change the course of human history.

The New Song

At this point I need to do a bit of summing up and drawing together of the various strands of the story I have been relating in this chapter. I have obviously been engaging in some speculative lines of thought but all of them originate in ideas that Jesus spoke about.

I have taken Jesus' idea of yeast and combined it with his other idea of stonework. I have shown that the Tabernacle, the earliest biblical model of a house of prayer, fits comfortably with this composition. I have then taken the three different aspects of Jesus' final instructions to his original group of apostles, the Great Commission, and used this in conjunction with the yeast, the masonry and the Tabernacle to underpin the idea of a three-step journey from the outside world into the heart of the kingdom. The ultimate goal of that journey is to become a spiritual warrior, an intercessor, a priest who can access the presence and call down the power of God on behalf of others and a king who can do battle with the forces of darkness in the world. Finally I have linked all these thoughts to the prophetic insights of John in the book of Revelation. There is evidence in the Gospels that Jesus anticipated these prophetic ideas but the consideration of that subject will best be left until we reach that part of the story.

Throughout the two thousand years of church history, by whatever means were made available by willing humans, or even by those who were unconscious of what was going on, the Holy Spirit has been hiding the yeast in the three measures of meal. We must be getting close to the point where the yeast has penetrated every part of human society, geographically, demographically and culturally. The infrastructure is in place for a worldwide house of prayer for all nations, a network of intercessory discipleship cells to complete the work of leavening the three measures of meal. The Holy Spirit-inspired Tabernacle must be nearing completion. There must be prayer warriors trained and ready in every nation. The job could soon be completed. There are days when I catch, faintly in the distance, the strains of that new song. Can you hear it?

> *You are worthy to take the scroll, and to open its seals; for you were slain, and have redeemed us to God by your blood out of every tribe and tongue and people and nation, and have made us kings and priests to our God; and we shall reign on the earth.*[10]

Chapter 10

Mysterious Symmetries

In his book *Christianity – A Short Introduction* Keith Ward raises the question of what Jesus meant when he talked about the kingdom of heaven.[1] He suggests that there are three possible ways to understand this key aspect of Jesus' teaching:

1. As a military/political intervention to transform human society with the kingdom as a renewal of the Davidic monarchy, throwing the occupying Roman forces out of the land of Israel. In that Jesus stated the kingdom was "at hand" he would have been implying that this was going to happen very soon.

2. As an inward, spiritual renewal of the human heart whereby in a largely metaphorical sense the rule of God would be established in people's minds, a new covenant, written on the heart rather than tablets of stone (Jeremiah 31:33) and with a new community in human history (the church) indwelt by the Holy Spirit.

3. As a cataclysmic supernatural change in the nature of reality which would bring the present form of history to an end and usher in the Day of Judgment.

I think we have already seen enough to make up our minds about the first possibility. At the beginning of his ministry Jesus may have been sorely tempted to go down the road of armed conquest but he rejected it and at the end of his ministry he told Pilate that his kingdom was not of this world and that his servants would not be taking up arms.[2] Despite the way in which those who, claiming to be his followers, have subsequently chosen that violent pathway there is nothing Jesus said that would support the idea of the kingdom of God being established by physical force. Yet the allusion to David's kingdom in Gabriel's announcement to Mary the mother of Jesus[3] suggests the operation of some kind of power and authority and therefore, perhaps, the importance of warfare in the spiritual realm.

We have, on the other hand, seen much in Jesus' teaching that gives full support to the second scenario, the inward spiritual renewal. We have devoted considerable space in this present study to finding out about how the indwelling Holy Spirit brings real change to the human heart from the inside, turning sinners into saints and equipping them to become spiritual warriors. In this we can see a fulfillment of Jeremiah's vision for the establishment of laws that are not written on tablets of stone but embedded in the psyche.

The Regeneration

That leaves us with Keith Ward's third proposal to consider, the regeneration, the second coming, a cataclysmic and supernatural transition into a new kind of reality. I believe the evidence points clearly to this also being on Jesus' agenda. During the third and final year of his ministry, and particularly in his last week in Jerusalem, Jesus prophetically set forth his ideas about the course that the kingdom would take in the future. He talked with his disciples about the end of the age and the events that would herald and attend its coming. He also gave some indications about the time that would elapse before the end of the age happened.

Now I realize I am getting into deep water here. It would be so much easier to go with the scholastic flow and see the Gospel writers attributing prophetic words to Jesus after the traumatic events that ensued when Rome finally got fed up with Jewish rebellion and put the boot in. But if that is what happened then the writers were naively creating a rod for their own backs. Why make it sound as if Jesus really did believe in "the end of the age"? I think we have to take him seriously.

Let us pick up the story on Palm Sunday at the beginning of Holy Week. After the triumphal entry into Jerusalem Jesus visited the temple and looked around at what was going on. He then returned to Bethany for the night. The following day on the way back into the city he cursed a fig tree for its lack of fruit and by the following morning it had withered away. Then for the second time in his ministry he cleansed commercialism from the temple, declaring that God's house of prayer was being made into a den of thieves. The temple then became the venue for a confrontation with the religious leaders and the telling of three parables: the Two Sons, the Wicked Vinedressers and the Wedding Feast.[4]

- A man had two sons, each of whom he asked to go and work for him in his vineyard. One agreed, but did not fulfill his promise. The other declined, but subsequently changed his mind and did the job. "Which of the two", asked Jesus, "did the will of his father?" His audience of religious leaders, quite rightly answered that regardless of his initial attitude and his words the one who actually went and worked in the vineyard obeyed his father's wishes.

- A landowner created a well-appointed vineyard and leased it out to others to tend while he traveled to a far country. At harvest time he sent servants to receive the fruit. These were abused and some of them even killed by the tenants. Finally he sent his son whom the tenants killed. The owner then returned, destroyed the wicked vinedressers and handed the vineyard over to others whom he could trust to exercise proper stewardship and deliver the harvest to him.

- A king arranged a marriage feast for his son and sent servants out with invitations. The recipients declined. So he sent more servants, but they too were dismissed out of hand. Some were abused and even killed. Naturally the king dispatched soldiers to punish those murderers. He then sent more servants to go and invite the general population. By this means he filled the wedding hall with guests.

Taken together with the enacted parable of the withered fig tree and the cleansing of the temple, Jesus is telling us through these three stories that the nation of Israel would cease to be God's agent of the kingdom. This was because of the failure of their leaders to repent of bad choices. As a consequence the responsibility and privilege of delivering the harvest would be given to another "nation".

Chosen Ones

Jesus then left the temple and went onto the Mount of Olives. Prompted by his startling prediction that the temple was going to be totally destroyed, Peter, James, John and Andrew came to Jesus with two questions:

- When will these things be?
- What will be the sign of your coming and the end of the age?

Jesus addressed the second question first. He foretold a period of wars, earthquakes, famines, pandemics and persecution of his disciples. False prophets would arise to deceive many and lawlessness would abound. Eventually there would be a period of great tribulation with the light of the sun and moon being blocked out and meteorites catastrophically colliding with the earth. Such would be the signs of his coming and the end of the age, and while all this mayhem is happening the gospel of the kingdom would be preached to all nations and the Holy Spirit would be powerfully present to orchestrate and inspire the communication of the message.

It was during this discourse that Jesus drew attention to a particular group of people, the elect or chosen ones – the Greek word is *eklektos* meaning *chosen* – who will play a key role during the end times. Five times in the Synoptic Gospels Jesus refers to this group of people.

The elect are a relatively small sub-group within the main body of disciples (Matthew 22:14 cf Luke 6:13) and their ministry is to cry out to God day and night (Luke 18:7). Jesus told a parable about a widow getting justice from a lazy and uncaring judge by pestering him to distraction to teach us about the key intercessory role of the elect during the period of widespread deception and faithlessness that precedes his return at the end of the age. The elect, although sorely tested, are the only ones who are not deceived (Matthew 24:24 & Mark 13:22). They are located in every part of the world (Matthew 24:31 & Mark 13:27) and it is on their account that the dark days of the end time are shortened (Matthew 24:22 & Mark 13:20).

In summary Jesus told us five things about these particular disciples:

- They will be relatively few in number
- They will be scattered throughout the world
- They are "round-the-clock" intercessors
- They will not be deceived by the false prophets
- Through them the great tribulation will be shortened

In the previous chapter we examined the Christian path of discipleship. The ultimate goal for a disciple is to become a prophetic intercessor, a prayer warrior, chosen and equipped to intervene via the spiritual realm in order to bring about beneficial results in the world of humanity. This group of people, represented in the book of Revelation as 144,000 in number, plays a crucial role in the endgame of human history. It seems to me that Jesus, in his description of "the elect", is drawing our attention to them.

Does it mean that there will be exactly 144,000? I doubt it. The number is symbolic as is also the reference to the twelve tribes of Israel in Revelation chapter seven. If we translate the twelve tribes of the old covenant into the new international spiritual nation that, according to Jesus, is to deliver the fruit of the kingdom to the returning owner of the vineyard, [5] then these chosen ones will be selected from every part of that worldwide nation. The twelve tribes represent the worldwide church and the 144,000 represent a guerilla army of spiritual warriors drawn from every part of that church.

Now let us be clear. This selection, or election, is not about salvation in the sense of going to heaven when we die; that is decided on other grounds that we have already discussed. Nor is it about attaining superior rewards, more comfortable mansions or shiny medals, so to speak, in heaven. This is about becoming a fully functional servant of the King. It is about being drawn into the councils of God, about being entrusted with his knowledge, about being given challenging jobs to undertake and about the sheer joy of pulling off crucial victories. The goal of the elect is to deliver a great harvest of fruit to the owner of the vineyard when he returns from the far country.

The Fig Tree

Jesus then went on to answer the first question posed by the four disciples; "When will these things be?" He did so in the form of several parables, the first being that of the fig tree. We need at this point to remind ourselves that shortly after Jesus' triumphal entry into Jerusalem he caused a fig tree, often a symbol for Israel in the Old Testament, to wither because it had no fruit. In so doing he illustrated the way in which Israel was going to lose its central role in the establishing of the kingdom, a message that he confirmed shortly after by telling the chief priests and elders that the kingdom would be taken from them and given to a nation producing the fruits of it. Keeping that in mind consider now the Parable of the Fig Tree:

> *Now learn this parable from the fig tree: When its branch has already become tender and puts forth leaves, you know that summer is near. So you also, when you see all these things, know that it (he) is near, at the very doors. Assuredly, I say to you, this generation will by no means pass away till all these things are fulfilled.*[6]

These are Matthew's words. Mark has almost the same [7] but Luke adds an additional detail:

> *Look at the fig tree, and all the trees. When they are already budding, you see and know for yourselves that summer is near. So you, likewise, when you see these things happening, know that the kingdom of God is near.*[8]

Within a few decades of Jesus' lifetime the nation of Israel ceased to exist and did not reappear until 1948. The second half of the twentieth century saw not only the re-emergence of Israel ("the fig tree") but also, on a wave of nationalistic fervor, a host of other sovereign states ("all the trees") coming into existence or re-emerging after a time of imperial subjugation.

I reckon that Jesus was telling us that within the lifetime of people born during the age of those events the kingdom would be established. We do not know how far into the future he thought that would be but we can see the second half of the twentieth century and the first half of the present century as a possible time window. Of course, as Jesus immediately went on to emphasize, no one knows the day or the hour except the Father but he has indicated an age that we early twenty-first-century humans can identify as ours. There is, however, another view to consider.

This Generation

Jesus' reference to "this generation" could straightforwardly be taken to mean the people he was actually addressing at the time. These words, together with one other passage in the Synoptic Gospels that we will look at in a moment, have led some scholars to conclude that Jesus expected the consummation of the kingdom to take place within his generation. Certainly his disciples hoped that the kingdom would end Roman rule in the near future; right up to the last they were questioning Jesus about this possibility.[9] However, Jesus consistently played down the idea of either a military or immediate consummation of the kingdom. He said that his kingdom was not of this world and his servants would not be taking up arms.[10] On his final approach to Jerusalem, specifically to counter the idea that the kingdom would appear immediately, he told the parable of the minas, in which he pictures himself traveling to a far country to receive a kingdom.[11]

We must also allow for Jesus' intimate knowledge of the Old Testament with its many prophecies, starting from as early as Genesis 12, that God would bless the whole world through the Hebrew people. This authenticates Jesus' belief that the gospel would be preached to all nations and since that process was clearly going to take much longer than his lifetime, the culmination of the kingdom must have lain for Jesus in the distant future.

It is clear in the Synoptic Gospels that Jesus foresaw a worldwide potential for the gospel of the kingdom. We have already seen that Jesus predicted Mary's story would feature wherever the gospel was preached in the whole world and he reiterates in Matthew 24:14 and Mark 13:10 that the message would penetrate the whole world. All three Synoptic versions of the Great Commission carry an international imperative.

We do not know how big Jesus thought the world was but he probably knew that the Roman Empire contained many different nations and that its boundaries had to be defended against other races of people outside the empire that Rome had not managed to conquer. He would probably have thought of the population of the world in terms of the number of stars in the heavens.[12] Jesus' view of the eventual size and scope of the kingdom is conveyed by such statements as:

> *And I say to you that many will come from east and west, and sit down with Abraham, Isaac and Jacob in the kingdom of heaven.*[13]

All this seems clear, but there is one other statement that appears to imply that Jesus expected an early consummation of the kingdom. It is recorded, with slight variations, in each of the three Synoptic Gospels:

> *Assuredly, I say to you, there are some standing here who shall not taste death till they see the Son of Man coming in his kingdom.*[14]

> *Assuredly, I say to you that there are some standing here who will not taste death till they see the kingdom of God present with power.*[15]

> *But I tell you truly, there are some standing here who shall not taste death till they see the kingdom of God.*[16]

At first glance Jesus appears to be saying that his kingdom would "happen" within the lifetime of his listeners. However, when trying to understand the Scriptures the context is crucially important. We cannot always chronologically locate events in the Gospels but in this case we can. In each of these three accounts the next episode in the narrative is the Transfiguration. Matthew and Mark place it six days and Luke about eight days after Jesus made this announcement. I think that for Peter, James and John the experience of seeing Jesus transformed so that his face shone like the sun, his clothes gleaming with an unearthly whiteness standing talking to Moses and Elijah, two long-dead prophets from Israel's past, would have been an adequate fulfillment of Jesus' prediction. Three of his disciples had been granted a powerful preview of the age to come.

"After a Long Time"

So if I am correct in my interpretation then Jesus never said he was coming back soon. In fact he implied a considerable timescale before the fulfillment of God's plan. I think the Gospel records overall make clear that Jesus taught the kingdom would start immediately, grow covertly over time and reach a final overt conclusion many years after his time on earth. The next three parables confirm this. Jesus follows up the lesson of the fig tree with a strong emphasis on the importance of not relying on his return being a long time in the future but living each day as if it could be the last. The story of Noah serves Jesus as a springboard to some vigorous warnings about being unprepared, the first of which is contained in the Parable of the Faithful Servant and the Evil Servant.[17]

In this story Jesus compares the behavior of two servants. In each case their master gives them full responsibility for his household during his absence. The faithful servant properly carries out his task and is duly rewarded with full and permanent stewardship. The evil servant, on the other hand, takes advantage of the delay in the master's return and abuses his privileged position. He is severely dealt with by the master when he returns unexpectedly. This is followed by the Parable of the Wise and the Foolish Virgins.[18]

Ten maidens are attending a bridegroom. Five were expecting the bridegroom to arrive without delay and took no reserve supply of oil for their lamps. The others went prepared for a long wait. In the event, when the bridegroom finally shows up, the wise girls have enough oil left for themselves but insufficient to share with their unfortunate colleagues. Jesus concludes:

> *Watch therefore, for you know neither the day nor the hour in which the Son of Man is coming.*

In both these parables Jesus is telling us that the end of the age will be later rather than sooner but will arrive unexpectedly. He is alerting us to the twofold danger of either complacency (as with the evil servant) or underestimating the time that will elapse before his return (as with the foolish virgins). Jesus follows these with the Parable of the Talents reiterating that the time will be long and telling us how we should be occupying ourselves while we wait.[19]

A man about to set out on his travels places his fortune in the hands of three fund managers. The first receives five-eighths, the second one-quarter and the third one-eighth of the portfolio, each according to his ability. The first agent invests and doubles the five talents deposited with him; the second does likewise with his two talents. The third is unwilling to take a risk and locks his single talent in a safe deposit box.

Eventually, "after a long time", the traveler returns. The first two agents are commended for their efforts and rewarded with enlarged areas of responsibility. The third is given the left boot of fellowship into outer darkness and his portfolio is handed over to the first agent, because:

> *To everyone who has, more will be given, and he will have abundance; but from him who does not have, even what he has will be taken away.*

The message is clear: use it or lose it. While we await the return of the King we must occupy ourselves in investing and multiplying that with which we have been entrusted. We must not neglect our responsibility through any false sense of our own incapability. The Master knows our potential and has tasked us accordingly. There will be a day of reckoning when he returns, and this is the subject of the final Holy Week parable, that of the Sheep and the Goats.[20]

The Big Pop

Jesus speaks of his return in glory, accompanied by the angelic host, to sit on his throne and judge the nations. He likens this to a shepherd dividing the sheep from the goats. The sheep are those who have fed the hungry, given water to the thirsty, taken in the homeless, clothed the destitute and visited the sick and the prisoners. The goats are those who have not done these things.

We have already discussed Jesus' teaching on the subject of the final judgment and you will find some more thoughts on this topic in Appendix 7. What I would like to focus on here is the setting for that event – the end of the age – to which Jesus referred in each of the five Olivet parables and, of course on many other occasions. Did Jesus think that the present form of history would come to an end in some sort of cataclysmic supernatural event that would bring the kingdom to fruition?

I reckon the answer to that question is clear. Yes, Jesus did think exactly that. But is it possible, scientifically speaking, that there could be such a phase change in physical reality, a discontinuity in history?

First, let us remind ourselves how it all began, with the big bang. On that subject, Francis Collins, leader of the Human Genome Project, says this:

> *There is at least one, singular, exceedingly improbable, and profound event in history that scientists of nearly all disciplines agree is not understood and will never be understood, and for which the laws of nature fall completely short of providing an expla-*

nation.[21] (Francis Collins. *The Language of God*)

Let us try and get our heads around that. Scientists almost unanimously agree that we will never be able to explain the big bang. The Large Hadron Collider is enabling physicists to investigate the conditions that existed when the universe was a few zillionths of a second old but however far back we are able to push our knowledge of the beginning of physical reality we will never be able to say with certainty what caused it.

Furthermore, the laws governing the physical world that once seemed so tidy are proving to be enigmatic. The astronomer and mathematician, John Barrow, has put it this way:

The laws of nature are highly mathematical but very mysterious. You cannot see or touch them. There are mysterious symmetries in the universe. It is no coincidence that biologists like Richard Dawkins feel very uncomfortable with religion and unanswered questions that are dealing with the messy complexities of nature. Physicists are very used to laws of nature that have no explanation of the biological sort. They are used to dealing with uncertainty and being undogmatic. There is a real cultural difference between biologists and physicists.[22] (John Barrow quoted by Mandy Garner in *Infinities and Beyond*)

If something beyond the laws of physics was needed to kick-start the universe then could not that Original Cause bring it to a conclusion or a transition, a universal phase change that transforms the fundamental nature of reality? If it all began with an inexplicable "big bang" could there not also be an unpredictable "regeneration", to use one of Jesus' words? Ninety-four percent of the universe consists of dark matter and energy. Maybe what we can observe at present is only the chrysalis undergoing metamorphosis and one day there will be a "big pop" that gives birth to the butterfly.[23]

Deeper Magic

We are given some clues to this transformation in the resurrection body of Jesus. He looked the same although subtly different in a way that caused people to not immediately recognize him. He could get into a room without going through the door and he could disappear into thin air. Whether or not he still needed food, he was capable of eating. And his body still carried the wounds of the crucifixion. So he was physical but not with the same kind of physicality as us. He had undergone a transition.

Perhaps if we understood much more than we do, if we could actually grasp the ultimate laws of physics, then it would be possible to apprehend the supreme miracle of the resurrection of Jesus Christ in scientific terms that did not require the suspension or violation of those laws. This greatest of all miracles would be seen as an event that, although highly improbable from our point of view, was still consistent with the fundamental principles that govern the working of the universe. It seems to me that the One who invented quantum mechanics and who created chaos theory has enough ways to influence the course of events without needing to override the deepest laws of nature or violate human free will.

C S Lewis seems to be hinting at this in Aslan's explanation to Susan and Lucy of how it was possible for him to have been killed and come back to life again:

> *"But what does it all mean?" asked Susan when they were somewhat calmer. "It means," said Aslan, "that though the Witch knew the Deep Magic, there is a magic deeper still which she did not know. Her knowledge goes back only to the dawn of time. But if she could have looked a little further back, into the stillness and the darkness before Time dawned, she would have read there a different incantation. She would have known that when a willing victim who had committed no treachery was killed in a traitor's stead, the Table*

> *would crack and Death itself would start working backwards.*[24] (C S Lewis. *The Lion, the Witch and the Wardrobe*)

I find it fascinating to imagine that the answers to all possible prayers might have been pre-installed in the fabric of the universe to be tapped into by humans in ways that do not involve breaking the ultimate laws of physics. God is not some distant and indifferent potentate who needs to be "earnestly asked, entreated or beseeched" – all of which words feature in the Oxford Modern English Dictionary's benighted definition of praying – to intervene and do us a favor by overriding the laws of nature. My heavenly Father is the Founder Chairman of Kingdom Services plc, the originator of the lavishly resourced and intricately ordered enterprise that delivers the goods. He is, therefore, the ultimate source of all the blessings it is possible for me to enjoy. However, to access those blessings requires me as a son in the family business to learn the ropes, to understand more of the mind of God, to find out how to harmonize with the music of God, to discover the "different incantation" that has existed from before the dawn of time. I need to learn the new song.

When the Israelites had been without water for three days they came across a pool at Marah but the water was bitter and undrinkable. So Moses cried out to the Lord and the Lord showed him a tree. When this was thrown into the water it became drinkable. [25] The solution to the problem already existed; it just needed to be revealed, grasped and applied.

To access the goods requires human minds to connect with "the deeper magic", the "mysterious symmetries", the profoundest laws of nature that are the expression of God's compassion and generosity but are, at least for the present, inscrutable to us. Jesus has shown us how far a human can go down that road; the consummation of the kingdom is waiting for enough of us to learn how to follow him so that the "Jesus Effect" can become universal.

God's plan is to transform the entire earth into a place where righteousness dwells. This requires humans, the appointed rulers of the earth, to choose goodness for its own sake. Justice and peace will eventually dominate every living entity and every particle of inanimate matter. This will happen when men and women have learned to live in harmony with God and in concord with each other. As the nervous system of the planet we will transmit euphony into the deepest recesses of the creation and draw out from its bottomless mines the hidden treasures of health and wholeness and creativity that will underpin human welfare and happiness in an eternal dimension. When that happens God's kingdom will have come to fruition.

Chapter 11

The Day of the Lord

Some years ago I met and got to know the late Donald McPhail. I had heard of Donald many decades earlier in a tape-recorded talk by Duncan Campbell about the spiritual awakening that happened in the Hebrides – a group of islands to the west of Scotland – between 1949 and 1953. During that revival, Donald, then a young lad, featured notably as Duncan Campbell recorded in his pamphlet "The Lewis Awakening". At one particular meeting Campbell noticed Donald "visibly moved and appearing to be deeply burdened". He invited him to pray. "There was an immediate response and in that moment the floodgates of heaven opened, the congregation was struck by a hurricane of divine power, and many cried out for mercy". Such events seem to have been a feature of that period of intense spiritual renewal.[1]

When we met, some fifty years after that dramatic time, Donald and his wife Moraig were still faithfully engaged in home and overseas mission work and through them many others around the world had experienced the benefits of the Lewis Awakening. Traces of its legacy can also still be found in the local community. However, most of the original spiritual energy has now dissipated. Just over a century ago there was a similar awakening in Wales but there is now little left to show for it.

The history of Judaeo-Christianity is punctuated by stories of God moving with great power and amazing and far-reaching beneficial changes happening as a result. However, because we humans lack staying power, a process of decline sets in and the full force of the refreshing and creative work of the Spirit is dissipated within a generation or so. Only those involved at the start can fully grasp the experience. Others who come later may try to sustain the clarity and intensity but ultimately fail. God does not inhabit our gazebos.

Recycling Human Cock-ups

The greatest spiritual awakening the world has ever experienced flowed from the life and ministry of Jesus Christ, his death and resurrection, and the ensuing outpouring of the Holy Spirit at Pentecost. These happenings have had a more significant impact on the human race than any other historical events. To be sure the message has been reworked and contaminated and there have been some bad things done by flawed humans in the name of Jesus over the centuries but the overall effect has been beneficial and worldwide. Yet the kingdom of God has still not come to fruition.

It seems to me that the divine strategy must not only expect human failure but must also recycle it back into the plan to use it for our ultimate benefit. If any particular bunch of people can only be relied upon for a few decades at most before messing up then progress must be made in periods of about one generation. This is the only way in which God can achieve his long-term goal. Time is not of the essence for God; he dwells in eternity. His hope and enthusiasm and patience are boundless and he can afford to wait for however long it takes. The end result has got to be achieved through the willingness of the human race or it will not have the value to God that he desires. So, time and again he moves in power through human agents who make themselves available, building upon whatever good still remains from previous visitations of the Holy Spirit. As with the advance of the tide each wave recedes but is eventually replaced by one that travels higher up the beach.

The Bible makes clear that God's "Cunning Plan" has always accommodated human cock-ups. Anticipating our actions and recycling our mistakes is an essential component of God's creative love. For example, back in the days of the Judges the nation of Israel wanted a king. God tried talking them out of it because he, God, was their king but in the end he reluctantly let them have their way. After a dodgy start with Saul it worked well under David and for a time under Solomon but then, just as God had foreseen, it all went pear-shaped. However, some key features of the eventual kingdom of God were foreshadowed in that period. Many centuries later a descendant of King David was born in Bethlehem and the story was resumed. A string of human errors had been mopped up and reworked back into God's plan.

For another biblical example let us consider the rebuilding of the temple and the walls of Jerusalem under the leadership of Ezra and Nehemiah, recorded in the two books that bear their names. An intense spiritual revival empowered the nation of Israel as they were released from seventy years' captivity in an alien country to return to their homeland and restore the ruins of their capital city. They got the job done and there was great rejoicing but the spiritual fervor eventually faded away. Yet here, as with David and Solomon, some important features of the kingdom of heaven had been anticipated.

The World's Bestseller

The Bible, from which I have drawn these stories, has been and continues to be vital to the progress of Christianity. Yet actually this amazing book can be seen as another example of a God-inspired beneficial byproduct of human unreliability. God always expected us to make a religion out of a revelation and that contingency was factored back into the plan. God specializes in producing good results out of sub-optimal human choices and it seems to me that the Bible was just such a result. Let me explain.

I have argued that the guerrilla church model was what Jesus had in mind, a church composed of a network of symphonic cells without any kind of organizational superstructure such as Roman Catholic, Anglican, Baptist or Pentecostal to regulate behavior and provide cohesion. The linkage between the various parts was intended to come from the Holy Spirit working through the bonds of friendship and that, of course, is exactly how it happened in the early days.

Could such an unstructured church have composed the Bible? It seems to me that the Bible exists only because during the three hundred years after Jesus the church became institutionalized and moved away from the guerrilla model. Yet without the Bible I would have no source document on which to build a picture of Jesus and no basis for thinking that he intended his church to be as I have portrayed it. So let us take a look at how we came to have the Bible.

During Jesus' time the Old Testament, as we now call it, consisted of a number of separate scrolls with an index (lectionary) that every Jewish person learned by rote, rather like some of us were taught in Sunday school to recite the sixty-six books of the Bible. These were the Scriptures of the very early church. When Paul reminded Timothy that the holy Scriptures he had known from childhood were able to make him wise for salvation he was referring to the Old Testament. The early church never had the New Testament.

We can infer that in the early years strong oral traditions about Jesus came to be established. Then, as the church grew in size and the original apostles who had known Jesus approached their sell-by date, people began to write things down, letters to various churches or Christian groups, gospels and prophecies and these became widely circulated. There followed a process of research, collecting, thinking, discussing, editing and deciding by the network of leaders and teachers located in various churches around the Roman Empire, aware of and in touch with each other, albeit with a much slower speed of communication than today.

By the latter part of the second century the idea of a canon of scripture had become well established, largely to counter the influence of ideas that the majority of Christian leaders regarded as heretical. At this stage there was widespread agreement over all but a handful of the books that make up our New Testament. This needs to be emphasized because today some critics of the New Testament like to give the impression that it was the result of a shuffle-and-deal exercise carried out by a Roman emperor in the fourth century. In actual fact the New Testament was close to being a done deal more than a hundred years before Constantine got involved.

By 300 AD so much of the Roman Empire had been "infected" with the Christian message of forgiveness and love that the emperor Constantine decided Rome was never going to beat the Christians so they had better join them! By the end of the fourth century the Bible, containing both the Old and New Testaments, had been agreed in both the eastern and western branches of the church and today it continues to be the world's best-selling book. That is quite an accomplishment, but would it have happened without the Roman flair for getting things done?

Organized councils of church leaders took the decisions about what to include and what not to include in the Bible. I find it difficult to imagine how that could have happened if the church had continued to operate as it did in the early days. Of course, this can be seen either as evidence against my theory about the guerilla church model or supporting evidence for the idea that God has a strategy for recycling human aberration. For me the history of the church in the centuries that followed the composition of the Bible indicates that institutional Christianity was never going to be capable of fulfilling God's intention.

Like a Mighty Tortoise

Constantine's monopolistic liaison between church and state lasted for more than a thousand years and although there were countless godly men and women sustaining the witness to Christ throughout that period the established church became seriously compromised and corrupted. However, it was the Bible that eventually stopped the rot.

To God a thousand years are as a day. Coincidentally with western technology having progressed to the point that intercontinental travel was possible along came Martin Luther and the other reformers with the rediscovery of certain essential biblical truths. There is nothing quite like a bit of competition to stimulate market growth and over the last 500 years the two main brands of Christianity have slugged it out for market supremacy and thereby penetrated the remotest nooks and crannies of the planet. The Romans cornered the market in South America, the Protestants fared better in North America and Africa; and so on. Like a mighty tortoise moves the church of God, but brothers, we are not treading where we've always trod.

I have never baked bread so I needed to check a cookery book to find out that the yeast is first mixed up with water and sugar and this liquid is then blended thoroughly into the flour so that the yeast is dispersed into every part of the dough. Then the dough is left to rise as the yeast does its work. The reason for the careful mixing is that although yeast is good at multiplying it is not particularly mobile. (As a fungus, yeast is part animal, part plant in its behavior). So wherever there is one yeast cell there will soon be more yeast cells but if the dough has not been mixed thoroughly then there will be parts that do not have any yeast and those parts will stay unleavened. Whatever else they may or may not have accomplished the churches, over the past five hundred years have succeeded in distributing the yeast throughout the dough.

With all the imperfections of the past two millennia we have somehow contrived to reach the point where there is a worldwide infrastructure of two billion Christians and adherents of Christianity. Admittedly we are doctrinally and organizationally fragmented and we are still competing with each other but the Bible is now available in most countries and languages. With a final push Jesus' gospel of the kingdom, with its life-changing story of Mary's love and forgiveness, could soon be known all over the planet. A worldwide move of God in our generation could finish the job quickly enough that there would be insufficient time for us to lose the plot and screw up yet again. This could be the last time God is faced with having to recycle human unreliability.

Brokenness

There is in my library a slim book that has been there since 1963. Over the years I think I must have turned to it more times than any other in my collection. The language is quaint, some of its ideas are strange and the tone sometimes borders on the sanctimonious. However, its message is simple, powerful and highly relevant to our present theme. It is *The Calvary Road* by Roy Hession.[2] Those of my readers who are familiar with this mighty midget classic of Christian literature may already have detected its influence on some of the ideas in this book and an acknowledgement is heartily given. Of particular interest is that its themes are based on actual experience of a spiritual revival, in East Africa I think, that was sustained over many decades and not merely sudden, spectacular and passing as so many others have been. I recommend this book to anyone who has not yet come across it.

One of the key themes of *The Calvary Road* is "brokenness", a word that Hession uses as a synonym for "repentance". I would suggest that repentance is the central idea that has the ability to draw together the many strands of thought that have been generated by this study of the gospel of the kingdom as communicated in word and deed by Jesus of Nazareth. "Repent" was Jesus' first publicly uttered word recorded in the New Testament and it lies at the very heart of the gospel. As with Mary it is the very first step we take towards God and it accompanies every other step on our journey. Repentance allows even unbelievers to become as little children, unconsciously dependent on a heavenly Father. Repentance opens the door to the Holy Spirit, enabling us to work with God in purifying and developing our character and honing our choices. And upon repentance depends our qualification as a prayer warrior and as a spiritual judge who can do battle with the Canaanite giants.

Bringing Heaven to Earth

The prospect of being involved in that action is what excites and drives me. I was born in the decade that saw the fig tree of Israel blossom again. These are momentous times. We are now so close to telling Mary's story all over the world. The wave that will establish the full height of the tide could be approaching.

Furthermore, the world situation adds an element of urgency to this. Looked at from one point of view an enormous amount has been achieved in so many different aspects of human life. The trends in almost all determinants of human welfare and prosperity over the past century have been positive and our technology continues to advance. Yet intractable difficulties stem from human attitudes and motives that prevent us from justly distributing and enjoying the benefits of our progress. Crime, fundamentalist terrorism and economic meltdown all feed on that kind of selfishness and the lurking specter of climate change adds yet another potentially lethal threat to our future. The jigsaw pieces of the great tribulation that Jesus foresaw are falling into place.

Jesus was focused on the kingdom of God. The church, which he promised to build, is God's agent to the establishing of the kingdom. I have metaphorically pictured the church as the temple set at the center of the city and the city in turn as representing the kingdom. Individual repentant childlikeness, with or without intellectual knowledge or belief in Jesus Christ, secures ground floor citizenship of the kingdom. However, to participate fully in the redeeming and creative work of God requires progress beyond that point, and we have explored the Christian pathway of discipleship for those who seek to know more of God and to serve his purposes.

Unfortunately, the church started to drift off course from very early in its history, even within the period documented by the New Testament. The kingdom of God became confused with the church and the emphasis of the message of salvation shifted from "repentance" to "believing". The low profile and mobile network form of church organization modeled by Jesus, indicated in his teaching and symbolized in his parables was replaced by a geographically fixed congregational and hierarchical approach. Theology took the place of spontaneity and with theology came professional leadership and lines of demarcation both within the church and between the church and the rest of society.

This drifting off course turned into a major detour in the fourth century when Christianity was adopted as the Roman state religion. This has been partially corrected over the past five hundred years but the process of reformation needs to continue in the light of Jesus' teaching about the kingdom and the church if the job of bringing heaven to earth is to be completed. I have suggested that Jesus had in mind a guerrilla church, a network of small discipleship groups gathered around ascetic spiritual warriors.

Definitely Not a New Religion!

In making this suggestion I am not advocating another anthropocentric theological and ecclesiastical reconstruction. God forbid! Rather we need to focus on the historical record of Jesus' words and deeds while humbly entreating the Holy Spirit to move back in as Chief Executive. We must resist our tendency to elaborate and organize; we are not here to impress the world but to change it. We are to concentrate on being, and coaching others to be, prophetic intercessors. We must let Jesus build his church in the way he wants.

Nor am I saying that there is no value to institutional Christianity. The many good things that have resulted from the beneficial influence that the churches have had on all aspects of human society, even after due allowance for all the bad things, speaks for itself. And the churches continue to make a huge contribution to the spiritual and social health of the nations. Yet it feels as if there is something more to come.

God has a plan for the universe and that plan will come to fruition. He has built "mysterious symmetries" into the fundamental mathematics of reality, the "music" of physical existence, the "deeper magic" of consciousness. Like treasure hidden in a field the cosmos has the potential to be perfect as he is perfect. However, the system is set up in such a way that the creation itself, through the human race and led by the ultimate human, Jesus Christ, must discover the key to that transition. Freedom of choice is real. Yes, God is in control of everything and will achieve the eventual outcome he always had in mind but he does not set the exact course humanity will take in reaching the perfection of creative living. We have an important part to play.

The key is human repentance. This is the point at which the development of life on earth meets the mind and purposes of God. This is the place where our free will becomes reconciled with the will of God because we choose to choose what he wants. We come to realize that our best interests are served by willingly and completely obeying the promptings of the Holy Spirit even though we have the absolute freedom to do otherwise. When one particular person in a little country at the eastern end of the Mediterranean Sea about two thousand years ago based his entire life on that principle the world took a huge leap forward. The knock-on effects are still with us today but something else seems to be needed to complete the job. Perhaps we need to reach a tipping point; perhaps critical mass is required for the final chain reaction to get under way.

Critical Mass

I remember a particular Lower Sixth Form lecture on the subject of nuclear fission. After relentless interrogation by a classroom full of accomplished bomb makers A H "Hot Ass" Warburton, our much respected and totally unflappable chemistry master, gave way and explained that to create a nuclear explosion a 5kg sphere of the isotope 235 of uranium was required. Did we actually think we could go out and buy it at the local pharmacy? Well, in those days it was still possible to purchase the ingredients of gunpowder and other explosive materials over the counter so perhaps it was not a ridiculously forlorn hope.

Uranium atoms are constantly breaking down and emitting neutron particles. These escape into the atmosphere making uranium dangerously radioactive but not explosive, not that is, until there is enough uranium together in one place to form the critical mass.

A 5kg sphere of uranium is called the critical mass because on reaching this size and weight the rate at which neutrons are being fired off by spontaneous nuclear fission of atoms within the lump exceeds the rate at which they can escape from the lump. Ever increasing numbers of fast moving neutrons are trapped inside the lump causing a rapid multiplication of nuclear breakdowns. This results in an explosion with the release of enormous amounts of energy. That which had previously been dangerous becomes many times more dangerous when critical mass is reached.

In an atomic bomb the fissile material is carried as two hemispheres, each containing half of the critical mass, kept well apart until the moment of detonation. A conventional explosive is then used to impact them violently together fusing them into the critical mass that triggers the chain reaction capable of eradicating a major city and causing havoc over a wide area for years to come. Conversely that self-same reaction can be controlled beneficially in a nuclear power plant to energize thousands of homes and factories and schools and hospitals.

One human totally given over to finding and doing the will of

God in his life produced a chain reaction of forgiveness and love and creativity that has permeated and blessed the whole world in a way that no other person has done. Suppose that 144,000 people, or whatever number is thus symbolically represented, could be found scattered around the world, drawn from and representing every "tribe and tongue and people and nation". Let us suppose that these people have learned how to live in a way that is at least vaguely reminiscent of the level of harmony with God that was demonstrated by Jesus. Then let us suppose that they were to be linked together to produce critical mass. Might their prayers not trigger the "deeper magic", the latent potential for healing and regeneration embedded in the fabric of physical existence?

Paul seems to be suggesting this when he wrote:

> *For I consider that the sufferings of this present time are not worthy to be compared with the glory which shall be revealed in us. For the earnest expectation of the creation eagerly waits for the revealing of the sons of God. For the creation was subjected to futility, not willingly, but because of him who subjected it in hope; because the creation itself also will be delivered from the bondage of corruption into the glorious liberty of the children of God.*[3]

And Peter has a parallel thought:

> *But the day of the Lord will come as a thief in the night, in which the heavens will pass away with a great noise, and the elements will melt with fervent heat; both the earth and the works that are in it will be burned up. Therefore, since all these things will be dissolved, what manner of persons ought you to be in holy conduct and godliness, looking for* **and hastening** *the coming of the day of God, because of which the heavens being on fire, will be dissolved and the elements will melt with fervent heat? Nevertheless we, according to his promise, look for new heavens and a new earth in which right-*

eousness dwells.[4] (My emphasis)

A Little Child Shall Lead Them

The idea that God has set this whole thing up in such a way that humans have the responsibility, privilege and empowerment to finish the job both thrills me to bits and scares me to death. If we do not pull this off then some other people in the future will do so, but I want it to be in my lifetime. The prophetic indicator lights are switched on in a way that could not have been possible until this stage in our history. We believers have currently within our grasp the potential to release enormous blessings on our world. If we do not then many centuries of good work could be undone in a crusade of devastatingly destructive selfish madness.

Now the last thing I want to do is second-guess the Holy Spirit. So please take what follows in the next couple of paragraphs as something not much better than mathematical speculation with maybe just the faintest possibility of a grain of prophetic insight. Or maybe it's rubbish. You must be the judge.

In 1949 two octogenarian sisters, one of them blind and the other crippled with arthritis, prayed into existence a spiritual revival that spread outwards to touch about twenty thousand people. (That is the population of Lewis-Harris, the main island, and the center of the Hebridean revival.) Of course, Peggy and Christine Smith would not have been the only people concerned for or praying about the social and spiritual state of the Outer Hebrides at that time but the historical records credit them with the special prophetic intercession that triggered the events of 1949-1953 and produced a ten thousand multiplication factor. (Twenty thousand divided by two.)

Any quantity of uranium is dangerous but a lump containing critical mass is cataclysmically explosively dangerous. Jesus says that where two or three symphonically related believers pray together he is present with them and the Father will give them what they ask for. Clearly that happened in Lewis in 1949, with a ten thousand times multiplication factor. But this was only dangerous "uranium"; it was well below critical mass. What would happen if 144,000 symphonically related prophetic intercessors, strategically placed across the surface of the planet, were to be orchestrated by the Spirit of God to simultaneously pray a prayer to the effect of, "Your Kingdom Come"?

Factor in the ten thousand multiplier and you are up to 1.44 billion. That is already one-fifth of the Earth's population. (7.2 billion and counting.) So all we would need to complete the job and bless every person on Earth is a further multiplication factor of five. The added effect of critical mass, when uranium suddenly switches from being just dangerous to become devastating, should be more than enough to give us that extra boost.

If you think that my analysis may not be total rubbish and you are joining me in sensing there may be truth in these things then what should we do? I think we should make every effort to add to our faith the strength of character that will enable us to handle profound insight into the mind of God. Let us focus on learning ever more self-control under the gentle influence of the Holy Spirit's conviction of sin, righteousness and judgment. Let us try to increase the level of childlike faith in our heavenly Father on a minute-by-minute basis each day.

Let us try practical experiments in being guided by the Holy Spirit. We could start with things that are important to us but do not affect other people if the experiment fails. For example, I have recently started to use this approach in my solo mountain excursions with some interesting results.

Then let us be alert to the Spirit of God moving to form relationships between people of like mind and heart, folk who really feel they can relate closely to each other and pray together. I don't know how that will happen for you. It may come through the normal ways that friendships develop. Or it may be something out of the blue. I have experienced both. Those groups will need to be interconnected with other groups so some of us will be called upon to be the linkages between groups separated by culture, by nationality, by denomination, and even by religion and by distances ranging in scale from cross-town to intercontinental. The important thing is to learn how to follow the Father, to be sensitive to the promptings of the Spirit and to use our God-given tools of inner peace and repentance to stay on track.

In this way the Holy Spirit could build a network of friendship and prayer that embraces and enfolds the entire planet. There really could be in the world 144,000 people, or whatever number is thus symbolically represented, that God wishes to guide to a lifetime goal of forming a spiritual choir that can learn the new song. If you doubt that the Holy Spirit can do that sort of stuff then read the Acts of the Apostles and then *The Lewis Awakening* by Duncan Campbell.

To round off this journey through the kingdom gospel of Jesus let us return to where it all started, the house in Bethany where Mary, Martha and Lazarus lived, the house that was completely filled with the wonderful perfume of spikenard oil on the day when Mary anointed Jesus.

Now in the early twenty-first century is the time for supping love and for serving love but especially for spikenard love. We need to be surrendering ourselves totally in adoration, because it is in adoration that we will find the power to act. Here we may grasp our golden incense bowls and join the prayers of all the saints that rise like sweet perfume into the throne room of heaven.

Spikenard love will fill us with a passionate hunger for God in Christ generating empathy with the pain of others and an overwhelming desire to heal them and give them joy. Through this will flow the creative word of power that can change the world and consummate the kingdom. Heaven might be only a "brain-flip" away from where we are, perhaps hidden from our eyes in the dark matter and energy that fills most of our universe.

For that glorious transition to come about requires the worldwide band of prophetic intercessors to join forces under the direction of the Holy Spirit, to sing the new song that they alone can learn and experience with new force the eternal wisdom that was embodied in Jesus. If those whom God is calling can manage to do this then they will be able to come as little children to their Father and, taking his hand, go out to tame and lead in peace the spiritual leopards, lions and wolves that are terrorizing and savaging our world.

Epilogue

Let us take stock of our journey, our search to rediscover Jesus and his gospel.

- In chapter 1 we made a quick survey of the basis of belief systems. In particular we looked at the implications of Jesus' gospel for those folk who do not believe in God and how those of us who do believe should relate to unbelievers.

- In chapter 2 I made the case for the joined-up version of Mary's story, to be the essential accompaniment to the gospel of Jesus. In retelling it I hope to have done something towards propagating it afresh in the third millennium.

- In chapter 3 I argued, from Mary's story, that the most fundamental aspect of the character of God and therefore of Jesus' gospel is love. This love has a two-way cause-effect relationship with forgiveness and forgiveness is closely associated in Jesus' gospel with healing.

- In chapter 4 we unpacked faith, drawing on the personal experience and teaching of Jesus to show that each of us needs to rediscover childlike dependence on our heavenly Father in order to reverse the effects of the Fall and find a pathway to healing and service.

- Chapter 5 explored sin, repentance and the work of the Holy Spirit in enabling us to get free from sub-optimal behavior, to renew our minds and to hone the acuity of our choices in life. We looked at the important role that inner peace plays in this process.

- We then continued in chapter 6 to look at the other main aspect of the work of the Holy Spirit: spiritual warfare. We tried to understand how we could become active in the battle to defeat evil and extend goodness in our world.

- In chapter 7 we took this theme forward as we studied the Lord's Prayer. We entered the holy ground of worship and explored our calling to be prophetic intercessors, active agents of the kingdom and we surveyed the kind of training process we will need to go through.

- Chapter 8 introduced the corporate dimension of Christianity and I argued that Jesus' intention for the church is to be a house of prayer for all nations, the spiritual temple at the heart of the kingdom.

- In chapter 9 we continued the theme of collective Christianity with a study of yeast, another of Jesus' pictures and we saw how this combines effectively with his stonework model of the church and the Old Testament Tabernacle. We noted how these various models reveal a path of individual progress into greater levels of spiritual authority.

- The Easter week parables provided the framework for chapter 10. In these we focused on Jesus' teaching about the end of the age and the consummation of the kingdom and we identified its relationship to the present period of human history.

- In the final chapter I highlighted the cyclical or tidal nature of God's interaction with humanity, seasons of

> spiritual renewal followed by decline. Yet looking back over the history of Judaism and Christianity it is possible to see that overall there has been progress. In doing so we identified a challenge for Christians living in the early twenty-first century to seize a unique opportunity.

I find it reasonable to believe that if there is a God who has gone to the trouble of creating this world and placing humans, created in his image, within it then he has done so for a purpose. That he intends to share that purpose with us and seek our involvement and cooperation in bringing it about is where I think the biblical evidence is leading.

Eschatology is not an exact science and I am well aware that many before me have tried and failed to predict the "end of the age", the "second coming" or, by whatever other label can be given to it, the cataclysmic event that will transform the world as we know it. I do not think I have fallen into that trap. Prophecy does not point to a precise and inevitable outcome predetermined by God and revealed to a few but to an opportunity within his purposes for all of us to grasp.

The journey continues!

Notes and references

Chapter 1

1. The subject of femininity in the Godhead will be dealt with in chapter 3
2. Daniel Dennett, *Breaking the Spell*, p303, Penguin, 2006
3. Hebrews 6:1
4. Matthew 18:2-6; Mark 9:36,37; Luke 9:47,48
5. John Robinson, *Honest to God*, p29, SCM Press, 1963
6. ITN 26 October 2008
7. Isaiah 57:15
8. At the time of writing the speed of the fastest computers is measured in petaflops. One petaflops is a million billion calculations per second. The Chinese supercomputer Tianhe-2 clocks up nearly 34 petaflops.
9. It is interesting that in the only detailed record of Paul preaching to a Gentile audience (Acts 17:30) the challenge he delivered was, "God commands all men everywhere to repent."
10. Matthew 28:17
11. Luke 24:46,47
12. Bjorn Lomborg, *The Skeptical Environmentalist*, p48, Cambridge University Press, 2001
13. Revelation 21:22
14. Matthew 25:31-46
15. Matthew 7:21
16. Hebrews 11:6

Chapter 2

1. Each of the four Gospels contains an account of a woman anointing Jesus with perfume while he was eating a meal as a guest in someone's house. (Matthew 26:6-13; Mark 14:3-9; Luke 7:36-50; John 12:1-8)

There are some similarities in the records (they all mention perfume and set the incident in a dining room). However, Matthew, Mark and John place the incident in Bethany, a satellite of Jerusalem, during the last week of Jesus' life whereas Luke places it in Galilee, eighty miles to the north, at a time when John the Baptist was still alive in prison, that is about eighteen months before Jesus' death. So we have significant differences in both time and place between Luke and the other three evangelists and this divergence continues right through the details.

Matthew, Mark and John report that the perfume was very costly, that one or more of those present objected to the waste of such an expensive perfume because it could have been sold and the proceeds used to help the poor, and that Jesus told them to leave the woman alone because she was preparing him for burial and that they could help the poor at any other time.

Luke's account contains none of these particulars. He reports a dinner table conversation but on a totally different subject, and makes no mention of the perfume being extremely valuable or the objections to its waste. He also reports that the woman "was a sinner" whereas this was definitely not the case in the other three records. Luke's Gospel generally shows evidence of independent research and his preface implies that he visited Israel and interviewed eyewitnesses. His forensic approach marks him out as a serious historian. So it is clear beyond any reasonable doubt that two different incidents were being reported.

2. Mary's possession of an unopened flask of perfume worth more than a year's wages is consistent with her having been an "up-market" prostitute and with what is known about the

morality of some religious leaders at the time. This woman would have been serving wealthy clients and expensive presents were to be expected.

3. The Greek text, contrary to some English translations, does not contain the words "she bought it". Mary did not rush out and spend £15,000 on a jar of perfume. Literally translated Jesus actually said, *"Leave her that to the day of my burial she may keep it."* The NIV translators have bitten the bullet and run with the implication in these words that not only was the spikenard in Mary's possession some time prior to the anointing but that Jesus was aware of its existence and her intention for its eventual use. In the NIV translation Jesus says, *"It was intended that she should save this perfume for the day of my burial."* Given that the earnings of prostitution were condemned in both the law and the prophets (Deuteronomy 23:18 and Micah 1:7) it is likely that Mary, if she were the transformed Galilean prostitute, would have confided in Jesus about the spikenard at some time in their friendship, and it would have been consistent with his ideas about making use of unrighteous mammon that he should have suggested what Mary might do with it. In this way the earnings of prostitution were disposed of but were also redeemed, as she herself had been, by an act of love.

4. Matthew 10:3
5. Matthew 21:31,32

6. In relation to the Bethany (i.e. the second) anointing the three accounts of what happened agree on everything except one detail. Matthew and Mark say that the woman anointed Jesus' head whereas John says that Mary anointed Jesus' feet and wiped them with her hair. Of course, the head was the normal place to anoint someone and I am sure that Matthew

and Mark are correct in reporting this. However, an eye for detail is a feature of John's writing and revisiting the Jesus stories some years after the other three evangelists, he often fills in the gaps they have left. It is worth noting that the very large quantity of spikenard (one pound, according to John) would have been more than enough to anoint both head and feet.

Not once but twice John tells us that Mary anointed Jesus' feet and wiped them with her hair. It seems that John is emphasizing the unusual features shared by the anointing in Galilee and the anointing in Bethany. When the prostitute came to the dinner party unannounced, unwelcome and overcome with guilt and shame the closest she dared come to Jesus as he reclined on a couch at the table was his feet. She washed them with her tears, dried them with her hair and anointed them with perfumed oil. When, a year and a half later she came to Jesus, burdened by the thought of his impending death, she quite properly anointed his head. Then in memory of that earlier occasion she also anointed his feet and wiped them with her hair. Why else would she wipe his feet? In Galilee she had been weeping tears onto Jesus' feet and she needed to dry them before anointing them. But at Bethany there was no mention of tears and in any case Mary wiped Jesus' feet after she had anointed them. This unusual sequence of actions looks very like a re-enactment of the earlier occasion.

7. Matthew 26:13
8. Acts 20:35; 1Corinthians 9:14. In fairness to Paul he never met Jesus in the flesh and the Gospels had not been written.
9. 1Corinthians15:1-4

Chapter 3

1. Luke 7:36-50

2. C S Lewis, *The Cosmic Trilogy*, p327, Pan Books, 1989
3. Ephesians 5:25-33
4. Revelation 21:1,2
5. *Her sins, which are many, are forgiven,* ***for*** *she loved much.* Apparently the normal meaning of the Greek translated here as "for" is "because". It would usually mean that what follows it in the sentence is the reason for, or the cause of, what precedes it. So that would confirm the idea that Jesus is saying that love can cause or bring about forgiveness. However, we do need to be a little bit careful because there are some occasions in the New Testament, including a couple elsewhere in Luke (4:36; 8:25) where it is used as a weaker, non-causal link word. The translators of the New Revised Standard Version, for example, have decided to run with this weaker sense:

Therefore, I tell you, her sins, which were many, have been forgiven; ***hence*** *she has shown great love.*

But were they right to do so? I find it interesting that they appear to have been challenged by the ambiguity in Jesus' words but I think they were wrong to try and get rid of it. I do not think it is a good idea to gloss over this double meaning as the NRSV translators have done because the tears and the perfume and the kissing clearly preceded Jesus telling her that she was forgiven. Something subtler is going on here. The expression of Mary's love for Jesus came first; the announcement of her forgiveness came afterwards.

6. Proverbs 10:12; 1Peter 4:8
7. Mark 12:30,31
8. Matthew 9:1-8; Mark 2:1-12; Luke 5:17-26
9. There is further support for this close link between forgiveness and healing in another well-known story. The

parable of the sower features in all three Synoptic Gospels and all three record Jesus quoting from Isaiah 6:9,10. Luke 8:10 gives a much-abbreviated quotation but Mark 4:12 gives more of the original and Matthew 13:14,15 includes all of Isaiah's words. It is the difference between Matthew and Mark that I wish to highlight. Mark ends his quotation from Isaiah with the words *"lest they should turn and their sins be forgiven them"* whereas Matthew's version ends with the words *"lest they should understand with their heart and turn, so that I should heal them."* Matthew is quoting accurately from the original words of Isaiah – Isaiah used the word "heal" – but Mark has changed "heal" into "forgive". There is no way of telling whether Jesus made this change or Mark but Jesus, or someone close to Jesus, regarded the words as interchangeable.

10. John 21:25

Chapter 4

1. Now published in a book: Justin L Barrett, *Born Believers,* Free Press, 2012
2. Hebrews 11:1
3. John 14:12
4. Philippians 2:7,8
5. Matthew 18:1-6; Mark 9:36,37; Luke 9:46-48
6. Mark10:14-16
7. Genesis 3:6
8. Genesis 3:22,23
9. John 2:22

Chapter 5

1. Richard Dawkins, *The God Delusion*, pp.222-226, Bantam, 2006
2. Francis Collins, *The Language of God*, pp.21-24, Pocket Books,

2007
3. http://en.wikipedia.org/wiki/Aberfan_disaster
4. *The Quotable Churchill*, p106, Running Press, 1998
5. Matthew 4:17
6. Matthew 9:13, 11:20; Mark 2:17; Luke 5:32, 10:13, 15:7, 24:47
7. Hebrews 4:15
8. John 16:8-11
9. Matthew 18:1-5; 19:1-12,23,24
10. Matthew 15:19; Mark 7:21,22
11. Matthew 26:28
12. Luke 22:42
13. Matthew 26:53
14. Hebrews 5:7,8
15. Romans 5:19
16. Philippians 2:9-11

Chapter 6

1. Isaiah 11:6
2. Some have suggested the lion was stupid or mentally sick. Perhaps so. But then Robert Schumann and a number of other outstanding composers suffered from mental illness. It has also been suggested that the lion was merely playing with its prey as a domestic cat will play with a mouse it has caught. A search on the Internet will turn up several cases involving more than one lion. In the case I observed it was not playing, it was mothering. It went on for an extended period and both animals were starving as a result. Only the intervention of another lion to kill the antelope ended the relationship.
3. Jeremiah 1:11,12
4. Ephesians 6:10-18
5. Luke 11:20-22
6. Matthew 12:28
7. Luke 9:1,2

8. Luke 10:1,9
9. Acts 8:6
10. Acts 1:6-8
11. Matthew 13:12
12. Matthew 13:52
13. 2Timothy 3:16 (The Message)

Chapter 7

1. Ernest Gordon, *Miracle on the River Kwai*, Collins, 1963
2. Matthew 6:9-13
3. Romans 14:17; Galatians 5:16-25; 1Corinthians 4:20; Colossians 1:13; Acts 14:22; 2Thessalonians 1:5; 1Thessalonians 2:12; Hebrews 12:28, 2 Peter 1:11; James 2:5; Revelation 11:15, 21:24
4. Revelation 21:1-3
5. Ephesians 1:9,10
6. Matthew 4:4
7. Genesis 1:3
8. Matthew 5:11,12
9. The Dalai Lama, *The Wisdom of Forgiveness,* p73, Hodder & Stoughton, 2005
10. 1Corinthians 10:13

Chapter 8

1. John 4:21
2. Matthew 16:18
3. Geza Vermes, *The Authentic Gospel of Jesus,* p362, Penguin, 2004
4. Matthew 7:24-27; Luke 6:46-49
5. Matthew 21:33; Mark 12:1
6. Matthew 23:29; Luke 11:47,48
7. Luke 12:18
8. Luke 14:28-30
9. Luke17:28

10. Matthew 26:61; Mark 14:58
11. John 2:19
12. Matthew 16:18
13. 1Peter 2:4,5,7
14. Matthew 21:13; Mark 11:17; Luke 19:46
15. Matthew 16:19
16. Luke 12:32
17. Matthew 18:18
18. Arthur Peacocke & Ann Pederson, *The Music of Creation*, p59, Fortress Press, 2006
19. Geza Vermes, *The Authentic Gospel of Jesus*, pp.384-385, Penguin, 2004

Chapter 9

1. Matthew 13:33
2. Ephesians 2:19-22
3. Exodus 31:1-5
4. Luke 24:46-49
5. Matthew 28:18-20
6. John 20:21-23
7. Acts 5:1-11; 8:9-25; 13:4-12
8. 1Corinthians 4:20
9. Alister McGrath, *The Dawkins Delusion*, p75, SPCK, 2007
10. Revelation 5:9,10
11. Hebrews 11:39,40

Chapter 10

1. Keith Ward, *Christianity – A Short Introduction*, p112, One World, 2000
2. John 18:36
3. Luke 1:32
4. Matthew 21:28-32; Mark 12:1-12; Luke 14:16-24, 20:9-19
5. Matthew 21:43
6. Matthew 24:32-34

7. Mark 13:28-30
8. Luke 21:29-31
9. Acts 1:6
10. John 18:36
11. Luke 19:11-27
12. Genesis 15:5
13. Matthew 8:11
14. Matthew 16:28
15. Mark 9:1
16. Luke 9:27
17. Matthew 24:45-51; Luke 12:42-48
18. Matthew 25:1-13
19. Matthew 25:14-30
20. Matthew 25:31-46
21. Francis Collins, *The Language of God*, p54, Pocket Books, 2007
22. Mandy Garner, CAM 58, p30, The University Of Cambridge, 2009
23. For those wishing to study the relationship between modern science and divine revelation Keith Ward's book *Pascal's Fire* provides an excellent survey with many references to other sources. (Keith Ward, *Pascal's Fire,* One World, 2006)
24. C S Lewis, *The Chronicles of Narnia*, p185, Collins, 1998
25. Exodus 15:22-25

Chapter 11

1. Duncan Campbell, *The Lewis Awakening,* p21, Rare Christian Books
2. Roy and Revel Hession, *The Calvary Road*, CLC, 1950
3. Romans 8:18-21
4. 2Peter3:10-13

Appendix 1 – Daniel Dennett on Spirituality

Let your self go. *If you can approach the world's complexities, both its glories and its horrors, with an attitude of* ***humble curiosity****, acknowledging that however deeply you have seen, you have only just scratched the surface, you will find worlds within worlds, beauties you could not heretofore imagine, and your own mundane preoccupations will shrink to proper size, not all that important in the* ***greater scheme of things****. Keeping that awestruck vision of the world ready to hand while dealing with the demands of daily living is no easy exercise, but it is definitely worth the effort, for if you can* ***stay centered, and engaged****, you will find the* ***hard choices easier****, the* ***right words*** *will come to you when you need them, and you will indeed be a* ***better person****. That is the secret to spirituality, and it has nothing at all to do with believing in an immortal soul, or in anything supernatural.*

The seven key elements of Dennett's analysis of spirituality are underlined:

1. Turn from self and self-interest,
2. Exercise humble curiosity,
3. Visualize the greater scheme of things, yet
4. Focus on the immediate.
5. Sound judgment will result, along with
6. Wise words and
7. Refined character.

Each of those insights finds strong support from Jesus as can be seen in the following quotations from Matthew 5:48; 6:28,29,34; 10:16,19; 16:24; 18:4:

1. *If anyone desires to come after me, let him deny himself, and take up his cross, and follow me.*

2. *Whoever humbles himself as this little child is the greatest in the kingdom of heaven.*

3. *Consider the lilies of the field… even Solomon in all his glory was not arrayed like one of these.*

4. *Do not worry about tomorrow. Sufficient for the day is its own trouble.*

5. *Be wise as serpents, harmless as doves.*

6. *Do not worry about how or what you should speak. For it will be given to you in that hour what you should speak.*

7. *Therefore you shall be perfect, just as your heavenly Father is perfect.*

Appendix 2 – Salvation, Repentance and Faith

There is within the Gospels some ambiguity as to whether Jesus taught that personal salvation or entrance to the kingdom comes about by "repenting" or by "believing". At one extreme is the Gospel of John, which has "believing" as a major theme. John uses the word "believe" (pisteuo) nearly 90 times, and more than half of these are attributed to Jesus. In contrast there is not a single occurrence of the word "repent" (metanoeo).

At the other extreme is the Gospel of Matthew where personal salvation is exclusively linked to "repentance". "Believing", or its cognate "faith" (pistis), is related specifically to healings, miracles and successful prayer. Mark and Luke have some ambiguity, but generally support the idea that faith is the key to prayer, healings and miracles, rather than salvation.

John's Gospel was written considerably later than the Synoptic Gospels and most scholars consider it to contain much more theologically reworked material than the first three Gospels. Even The New Bible Dictionary, coming from the conservative evangelical school, acknowledges this christological content of John:

> *John does not contradict the other Gospels but interprets the Person who is depicted in them. While the other Evangelists have given us a photograph of Jesus, John has given us a portrait. (NBD, Second Edition, Inter-Varsity Press, 1982)*

Although John is the least reliable of the Gospels as a source for the actual words of Jesus he fills in some of the gaps left by the Synoptic Gospels. The personal details in many passages ring true as history and his chronology is clearer. Moreover, on the one and only occasion when John deals specifically with entry to the kingdom (3:3,5) the route he defines is through *being born again… of the Spirit.* This closely parallels the teaching of Jesus in the Synoptic Gospels, that entry to the kingdom requires us to become as a little child. John has pushed this idea back to its logical source – spiritual rebirth.

To sort out the apparent ambiguities within the Synoptic Gospels I have listed below all the eighteen relevant texts according as to whether they link personal salvation or entry to the kingdom with the word "repentance" or with the interchangeable words "faith" and "believing".

Repentance alone

1. Repent for the kingdom of heaven is at hand. (Matthew 4:17)

2. I did/have not come to call the righteous but sinners to repentance.
   (Matthew 9:13, Mark 2:17, Luke 5:32)

3. And they… preached that people should repent. (Mark 6:12)

4. Then he began to upbraid the cities in which most of his mighty works had been done, because they did not repent. (Matthew 11:20,21)

Woe to you Chorazin! Woe to you Bethsaida! For if the mighty works which were done in you had been done in Tyre and Sidon they would have repented. (Luke 10:13)

5. They repented at the preaching of Jonah. (Matthew 12:41, Luke11:32)

6. Unless you repent you will likewise perish. (Luke 13:3,5)

7. More joy in heaven over one sinner who repents. (Luke 15:7)

8. Repentance and forgiveness of sins should be preached in his name to all nations. (Luke 24:47)

9. Unless you are converted (turn) and become as little children, you will by no means enter the kingdom of heaven. Therefore, whoever humbles himself as this little child is greatest in the kingdom of heaven. (Matthew 18:3,4)

Repentance with Believing or Faith

10. Jesus came to Galilee preaching the gospel of the kingdom of God, and saying, "The time is fulfilled, and the kingdom of God is at hand. Repent and believe in the gospel." (Mark 1:14,15)

Believing or Faith alone

11. Your sins are forgiven... Your faith has saved you. Go in peace. (Luke 7:48,50)

12. ...lest they should believe and be saved. (Luke 8:12)

13. Receive your sight; your faith has saved you. (Luke 18:42)

14. Go into all the world and preach the gospel to every creature. He who believes and is baptized will be saved but he who does not believe will be condemned. (Mark 16:15,16)

Nine of the fourteen texts unequivocally state that the headline message of the gospel of the kingdom is "repent". Any ambiguity arises from five texts, two in Mark and three in Luke. These are numbered 10 to 14 above.

Text No 10 In this passage Mark introduces Jesus preaching that the kingdom is at hand and calling for people to "repent and believe the gospel". The object of the faith demanded by the message is the gospel. The statement is, therefore, circular. It is stressing the importance of repentance. Since the cross and the Resurrection were still in the future at the time this message was being preached, Jesus could not have been calling for belief in those events. The fundamental message of repentance is amplified not attenuated by the call to believe the gospel.

Texts No 11, 12 and 13 are all in Luke and need to be considered together. Text No 13 is taken from the story of sight restoration to a blind man near the city of Jericho. Jesus effects this healing with the words:

Receive your sight; your faith has saved you.

In this instance the word "saved" means "healed". The man was being saved from the consequences of physical blindness. No other meaning is possible in the context. The man's faith was in God and in Jesus' ability to heal.

Against that background Jesus' words to Mary in the house of Simon the Pharisee (Text No 11) should be taken to mean that she had been saved from the consequences of prostitution. The physical and emotional damage was repaired and possibly she was healed from a sexually transmitted disease. Here also Mary's faith was in God and in the person of Jesus.

Text No 12 is found in the parable of the sower. The theme is receiving the word of God by faith and delivering the result that word was intended to produce. A careful examination of the context does not encourage the idea that "being saved" means anything other than it does in Texts No 11 and 13, i.e. deliverance from an adverse personal situation in the here and now.

That leaves just Text No 14. In this case it is clear that the final judgment and eternal salvation are the subjects in view, and "believing" is being asserted to be the key to moral exoneration at the end of the age. However, are these the genuine words of Jesus? This verse is located in a passage of dubious authenticity. The NRSV and NIV translations demote it to a footnote with the comment that the most reliable early manuscripts and other ancient witnesses do not contain it.

My conclusion is that of the five Synoptic texts that might be associating forgiveness or eternal salvation with faith, in four cases they are not actually doing so. In the fifth case the provenance is suspect. In no way do these texts overturn the otherwise clear teaching of the Synoptic Gospels that forgiveness and remission of sins is predicated on repentance.

Appendix 3 – Gender in the Godhead

In the beginning God created man in his own image; in the image of God he created him; male and female he created them (Genesis 1:27)

Humanity consists of two complementary halves and both are needed to express the image of God. In the alternative creation story in Genesis chapter two this comes about through separation; Eve is extracted from Adam's side. Humanity is bi-polar, its two parts different from and strongly attracted to each other. I am not suggesting that God's nature is related directly to human sexual orientation but that it is best understood by us as containing both feminine and masculine characteristics.

In my day job I often visit nursery and primary schools. The vast majority of teachers and head teachers I meet are women. Women and young children seem naturally to gravitate together, perhaps as an extension of the maternal bond. The Holy Spirit, according to Jesus speaking at the Last Supper, is the one who teaches, guides, comforts, reproves and brings all things to our remembrance. The Spirit also helps our infirmities and intercedes for us. Of course, men can do these things and some do them very effectively but women, on the whole, seem to do them particularly well with young children.

In character as well as activity the Holy Spirit also portrays feminine virtues. Andrew Murray has this to say on the subject:

The fruit of the Spirit is love. From that there come all the graces and virtues in which love is manifested: joy, peace, longsuffering, gentleness, goodness; no sharpness or hardness in your tone, no unkindness or selfishness; meekness before God and man. You see that all these are the gentler virtues. I have often thought as I read those words in Colossians, "Put on therefore as the elect of God, holy and beloved, bowels of mercies, kindness, humbleness of mind,

> *meekness, longsuffering," that if we had written, we should have put in the foreground the manly virtues, such as zeal, courage and diligence; but we need to see how the gentler, the most womanly virtues are specially connected with dependence upon the Holy Spirit.* *

As a man I appreciate and celebrate women – although I doubt I will ever fully understand them – and the difference between the genders. I believe this reflects in some way the nature of God and I find it helpful to visualize the Holy Spirit as the repository and exponent of femininity within the Godhead.

* Absolute Surrender, Andrew Murray, Bibliotech Press, 2012, p 21

Appendix 4 – Jesus Speaking about the Gospel

These are the eight occasions recorded in Matthew, Mark and Luke when Jesus used the word "gospel". (The word "gospel" does not appear in John, one of several interesting omissions from that book.) In these scriptures Jesus tells us a number of important things about his gospel. It is the good news about the kingdom of God, it is accessed through repentance and faith and healings of many kinds accompany its proclamation. The poor are its primary target audience and it will have been preached all over the world as a witness to all nations when this age comes to an end. The anointing of the Spirit of the Lord is essential to the task of preaching the gospel and those who take up this work will make personal sacrifices and suffer persecution. Major themes to be covered are deliverance to the captives, recovery of sight to the blind and the acceptable year of the Lord. However, the only piece of biography selected for inclusion is Mary's story.

1. The time is fulfilled, and the kingdom of God is at hand. Repent and believe in the gospel. (Mark 1:15)

2. The Spirit of the Lord is upon me, because he has anointed me to preach the gospel to the poor. He has sent me to heal the brokenhearted, to preach deliverance to the captives and recovery of sight to the blind, to set at liberty those who are oppressed, to preach the acceptable year of the Lord. (Luke 4:18,19)

3. The blind receive their sight and the lame walk; the lepers are cleansed and the deaf hear; the dead are raised up and the poor have the gospel preached to them. (Matthew 11:5 and similarly in Luke 7:22)

4. For whoever desires to save his life will lose it, but whoever loses his life for my sake and the gospel's will save it. (Mark 8:35)

5. Assuredly, I say to you, there is no one who has left house or brothers or sisters or father or mother or wife or children or lands, for my sake and the gospel's, who shall not receive a hundredfold now in this time – houses and brothers and sisters and mothers and children and lands, with persecutions – and in the age to come, eternal life. (Mark 10:29,30)

6. And this gospel of the kingdom will be preached in all the world as a witness to all the nations, and then the end will come. (Matthew 24:14 and similarly in Mark 13:10)

7. Assuredly, I say to you, wherever this gospel is preached in the whole world, what this woman has done will also be told as a memorial to her. (Matthew 26:13 and similarly in Mark 14:9)

8. Go into all the world and preach the gospel to every creature. (Mark 16:15)

Appendix 5 – Faith, Belief and Believing in the Synoptic Gospels

Here are the twenty-one occasions recorded in the Synoptic Gospels where Jesus speaks about "faith" or "believing". (These words are cognate in NT Greek).

1. And behold they brought to him a paralytic lying on a bed. And Jesus, seeing their faith, said to the paralytic, "Son, be of good cheer; your sins are forgiven."
   Matthew 9:2 and similarly in Mark 2:5 and Luke 5:20

2. "Now if God so clothes the grass of the field, which today is, and tomorrow is thrown into the oven, will he not much more clothe you, O you of little faith?"
   Matthew 6:30 and similarly in Luke 12:28

3. When Jesus heard it, he marveled, and said to those who followed, "Assuredly, I say to you, I have not found such great faith, not even in Israel!" – Then Jesus said to the centurion, "Go your way; and as you have believed, so let it be done for you." And his servant was healed that same hour.
   Matthew 8:10,13 and similarly in Luke 7:9,10

4. Then he said to the woman, "Your faith has saved you. Go in peace."
   Luke 7:50

5. But he said to them, "Why are you fearful, O you of little faith?" Then he arose and rebuked the winds and the sea. And there was a great calm. Matthew 8:26.
   Similarly in Mark 4:40 except "no faith" and in Luke 8:25 "Where is your faith?"

6. "Those by the wayside are the ones who hear; then the devil comes and takes away the word out of their hearts, lest they should believe and be saved. But the ones on the rock are those who, when they hear, receive the word with joy; and these have no root, who believe for a while and in time of temptation fall away."
   Luke 8:12,13

7. But Jesus turned around, and when he saw her he said, "Be of good cheer, daughter; your faith has made you well." And the woman was made well from that hour.
   Matthew 9:22 and similarly in Mark 5:34 and Luke 8:48

8. As soon as Jesus heard the word that was spoken, he said to the ruler of the synagogue, "Do not be afraid; only believe."
   Mark 5:36

But when Jesus heard it, he answered him, saying, "Do not be afraid; only believe, and she shall be made well."
Luke 8:50

9. And when he had come into the house, the blind men came to him. And Jesus said to them, "Do you believe that I am able to do this?" They said to him, "Yes, Lord." Then he touched their eyes, saying, "According to your faith let it be to you." And their eyes were opened.
   Matthew 9:28-30

Mark records a similar/different incident with one blind man called Bartimaeus in 10:52:

Then Jesus said to him, "Go your way; your faith has made you well." And immediately he received his sight and followed Jesus on the road.

And similarly in Luke 18:42:

Then Jesus said to him, "Receive your sight; your faith has saved you."

10. And he did not do many mighty works there because of their unbelief.
    Matthew 13:58

Now he could do no mighty work there, except that he laid his hands on a few sick people and healed them. And he marveled because of their unbelief.
Mark 6:5,6

11. And immediately Jesus stretched out his hand and caught him, and said to him, "O you of little faith, why did you doubt?"
    Matthew 14:31

12. Then Jesus answered and said to her, "O woman, great is your faith! Let it be to you as you desire." And her daughter was healed from that very hour.
    Matthew 15:28

13. But when Jesus perceived it, he said to them, "O you of little faith, why do you reason among yourselves because you have brought no bread?"
    Matthew 16:8

14. Then Jesus answered and said, "O faithless and perverse generation…"
    Matthew 17:17 and also Mark 9:19 and Luke 9:41

Then the disciples came to Jesus privately and said, "Why could we not cast him out?" So Jesus said to them, "Because of your unbelief; for assuredly, I say to you, if you have faith as a mustard seed, you will say to this mountain, 'Move from here to there,' and it will move; and nothing will be impossible for you. However, this kind does not go out except by prayer and fasting."

Matthew 17:19-21

Jesus said to him, "If you can believe, all things are possible to him who believes."

Mark 9:23

15. "But whoever causes one of these little ones who believe in me to sin (stumble), it would be better for him if a millstone were hung around his neck, and he were drowned in the depth of (thrown into) the sea."
    Matthew 18:6 & Mark 9:42

16. And the apostles said to the Lord, "Increase our faith." So the Lord said, "If you had faith as a mustard seed, you would say to this mulberry tree, 'Be pulled up by the roots and be planted in the sea,' and it would have obeyed you."
    Luke 17:5,6

17. And he said to him, "Arise, go your way. Your faith has made you well."
    Luke 17:19

18. "Nevertheless, when the Son of Man comes, will he really find faith on the earth?"
    Luke 18:8

19. So Jesus answered and said to them, "Assuredly, I say to you, if you have faith and do not doubt, you will not only do

what was done to the fig tree, but also if you say to this mountain, 'Be removed and be cast into the sea,' it will be done. And all things, whatever you ask in prayer, believing, you will receive."
Matthew 21:21,22

So Jesus answered and said to them, "Have faith in God. For assuredly, I say to you, whoever says to this mountain, 'Be removed and cast into the sea,' and does not doubt in his heart, but believes that those things he says will come to pass, he will have whatever he says. Therefore I say to you, whatever things you ask when you pray, believe that you receive them, and you will have them."
Mark 11:22-24

20. "But I have prayed for you, that your faith should not fail."
Luke 22:32

21. Afterwards he appeared to the eleven as they sat at the table; and he rebuked their unbelief and hardness of heart, because they did not believe those who had seen him after he had risen. And he said to them, "Go into all the world and preach the gospel to every creature. He who believes and is baptized will be saved; but he who does not believe will be condemned. And these signs will follow those who believe: In my name they will cast out demons; they will speak with new tongues; they will take up serpents; and if they drink anything deadly, it will by no means hurt them; they will lay hands on the sick, and they will recover." Mark 16:14-18

Appendix 6 – Brickwork Experiments

This experiment is designed to illustrate how the idea of a building made from interlocking bricks or stones ties in with the human relationships that Jesus developed within his closest group of disciples. It can be carried out with house bricks but children's toy blocks, matchboxes, DVD cases or books are easier to handle. You will need thirteen, all the same size. With house bricks you will probably need a second person or a few extra bricks to act as supports. DVD cases work particularly well because they are smooth and light. Each of these objects has six faces. This is obviously so with bricks. Books or DVDs are flatter but the four edges count as faces.

I will use the points of the compass to indicate directions in the plane of the floor or table on which the bricks are being built. North is away from you, south towards you and east and west right and left respectively. All bricks are to be placed with their largest face towards the table and with their longest dimension pointing east/west.

Start by laying down Brick 1. Then lay Brick 2 to the east of Brick 1 exactly in line with and touching Brick 1. The north-south line of their contact we will call the Middle Line. Lay Brick 3 to the north of and touching the first two so that its mid point lies on the Middle Line. Each one of these three bricks has face-to-face contact with the other two and there is a point at which all three touch each other. Now place Brick 4 on top of the first three so that its center lies directly above that point. You now have four bricks all touching each other face to face.

Now try placing a fifth brick so that it touches all these four. It cannot be done. Thus the first conclusion is that the maximum number of bricks that can touch each other face-to-face is four. This can be seen to parallel the inner group of Peter, James and John, who had a particularly close relationship with Jesus and each other.

The second stage of the experiment requires a degree of balancing but is easy to perform with DVD cases or books. First add three more bricks, numbers 5,6 and 7, in a third layer, exactly above Bricks 1,2 and 3. If you keep one hand pressing down in the middle, or place a weight there, they will stay in position.

At this stage you will have six bricks touching the middle brick; the original three are touching its lower face and the latest three are touching its top face. That leaves the four side faces of Brick 4, the central brick, not touching anything. Now add six more bricks to the middle layer as follows.

Add Bricks 8 and 9 respectively to the east and west of, exactly aligned with and touching Brick 4. Add Bricks 10 and 11 to the north so that they touch each other along the Middle Line and both are in contact with Brick 4. Finally add Bricks 12 and 13 to the south so that they touch along the Middle Line and are both in contact with Brick 4.

At this point you should be able to remove your hand without the pile collapsing. You now have twelve bricks all touching Brick 4, the central brick, face-to-face and there is no room for any more. From this we can conclude that twelve is the largest number that can gather around and relate to the one in the center. (Topologists will be able to find solutions greater than twelve but twelve is the most symmetrical solution. If identical spheres are substituted for rectangular blocks then twelve is the unique solution.)

Jesus' choice of twelve disciples as members of his intensive training group with an inner group of three should perhaps be seen as normative rather than prescriptive. I think it is reasonable that as a joiner working alongside and watching stonemasons at work Jesus would have reflected on how the strength of a building was achieved through this pattern.

Appendix 7 – The Sheep and the Goats

The manuscript of this book originally contained a chapter devoted to the seven parables of the kingdom as recorded in Matthew chapter thirteen that was entitled The Shoreline Seminar. Since this passage contains the greatest number of mentions of the kingdom of God in the whole of the New Testament it should really have been included in any serious study of Jesus' gospel of the kingdom. However, as I came to settle ever more certainly on prophetic intercession as the focal point for this book, a detailed analysis of the kingdom parables, with the exception of the yeast, became increasingly difficult to fit within the mainstream flow of the narrative.

I think the reason for this is that the Sermon on the Mount and the Shoreline Seminar each tell the story of the kingdom but using different approaches. The Sermon was to be understood, at least to some extent, by the general public whereas the Seminar was not. Integrating them into one narrative is fascinating and rewarding but complicated.

Reluctantly, therefore, I found it necessary to drop that chapter but I have managed to mention most of its material within the text except for the subject of the "wailing and gnashing of teeth" and the parable of the Sower. The latter is one of my favorites and I excluded it with great reluctance. However, its message, using different metaphors, is firmly embedded in the story. The former was, I felt, too important to omit from the book. What follows, therefore, is a compilation of the relevant parts of the deleted chapter.

Children by Choice

Some years ago my adult daughter and I were discussing the difference between the love of married couples and that of parents and children. I observed that except perhaps in certain cases of adoption neither children nor parents get to choose each other whereas marriage is a mutual choice. A day or so later she came to me and said that although she had not been able to choose me as her father, had she had that opportunity then she would have done so. I was deeply moved by her words. That another human, who knows exactly how moody, mean and grouchy I can sometimes be, should feel that way about me was humbling yet intensely fulfilling. Even more important was that it gave me a valuable insight into God's motivation in creating the universe and the human race.

If we do a reasonably good job as human parents then the natural instinctive love for and of our children will translate into lifelong friendships. We will not only have procreated our sons and daughters but we will have established a mutual loyalty and trust that stems from a different and independent kind of love. Our children will, in a sense, have opted into our family. It seems to me that God is looking to have many billions of individually unique children that are in his family by choice, beings that God has not only created but also adopted.

God's goal has always been a perfect creation. Before humans there were angels. It seems that these glorious creatures, although possessed of powers beyond those of our race, do not have the degree of free will that we have been given. They are wired up to serve God to the letter. Their only choice is to carry on doing what they were created to do or to opt out totally. They are either on God's team or they are in total opposition to God. There is a prophetic hint that one-third of the angels chose the latter course and thereby became the operational center for evil in the universe. [1] (That would make our world two parts good and one part bad, which feels about right to me.) However, God desired something more than angels.

God wanted children, and we humans have been created lower than the angels but with the potential to rise above them. [2] It seems to me that we are the treasure hidden in the field, the pearl of great price that Jesus spoke about in his parables. The crowning glory of the creation is intended to be a people made in God's image: they will be good because, like God, they have chosen to be good. In attaining that position we humans will have failed dismally on many occasions but we will have demonstrated an enduring commitment to be perfect just as our heavenly Father is perfect.[3]

We will have shown courage while being tempted towards cowardice, we will have exercised patience when time was short, we will have been kind when kindness was undeserved and we will have stayed meek when under intense provocation. In summary, we will have learned to love our neighbor as our self when love was not an easy choice.

However, it is inevitable that when goodness is a matter of choice not all will choose goodness. Two of the seven parables in Matthew chapter thirteen foretell that at the end of the age there will be a separation between the good and the bad. The tares will be separated from the wheat; the bad fish caught in the dragnet will be thrown away and the good fish retained. The destination for the weeds and the inedible fish is described as a furnace of fire wherein there will be weeping and gnashing of teeth.

There is no avoiding the fact that Jesus referred numerous times to this subject. He used several metaphors to describe the process of sorting out good from evil and their respective destinations. It is clear that he was using metaphor because some of the descriptions are contradictory; fire and darkness, for example, are mutually exclusive. Throughout the two millennia of Christianity we have tended to take his words literally in our teaching, writing and art and we need to make a conscious effort to step back from this picture language if we are to take an objective view.

It is particularly important to take a close look at precisely what or who is to be cast into the furnace of fire. Jesus mentions three groups of people:

- The sons of the wicked one
- Those who practice lawlessness
- The wicked (as opposed to the just)

But then, significantly, he adds a fourth category:

- All things that do offend[4]

The first three groups are living persons but the fourth group is something else.

The Refiner's Fire

In the Sermon on the Mount Jesus had described a world in which peace, justice, humility, meekness, honesty, tolerance and generosity dominate the behavior of humans. For that world to come into existence will require the separation and destruction of the opposites of those characteristics: aggression, injustice, pride, arrogance, deceit, bigotry and selfishness. These offensive aspects of human nature need to be dealt with. They need to be purged out of the human race. All things that do offend must be cast into the furnace.

Personally I find nothing strange about the idea that we humans should be called before God to give account of how we have lived our lives. The God I know is perfect and just and I would not want God to be anything other than perfect and just. I am flawed. My life has been a mixture of generally well-motivated and sometimes effective acts of love and kindness, many stupid mistakes, some of them serious, and a good deal of downright mean and deliberately bad behavior. That I should have to face up to all that and undergo intense examination and correction seems totally fair and reasonable. In all my waywardness, though, I yearn to be perfect and I reckon that billions of other humans feel the same. I believe that this longing comes to us from God, who loves and desires to perfect everyone.

So an important aspect of what Jesus has in view is the elimination of the offensive from inside us, the eradication of impure motives, bad attitudes and negative emotions that we have inherited or acquired from past experiences or deliberately or carelessly implanted within our hearts. This process will be focused not on our extermination or punishment but on our purification in order to adapt us for living in the environment of God's domain.

The prophet Malachi wrote about the day when the Lord would come like a refiner's fire to purify people as gold and silver is purified in the furnace. [5] Paul develops this idea in 1 Corinthians 3:11-15:

For no other foundation can anyone lay than that which is laid, which is Jesus Christ. Now if anyone builds on this foundation with gold, silver, precious stones, wood, hay, straw, each one's work will become manifest; for the Day will declare it, because it will be revealed by fire; and the fire will test each one's work, of what sort it is. If anyone's work which he has built on it endures, he will receive a reward. If anyone's work is burned, he will suffer loss; but he himself will be saved, yet so as through fire.

I have not studied Roman Catholic theology but I imagine that they would cite this passage in support of their doctrine of purgatory, a season of purification for the dead before they are allowed to enter heaven. Protestants generally reject that teaching but when one allows the Bible to speak for itself the idea behind it does not seem so unscriptural. Personally I would want to avoid building an elaborate doctrine out of it because I do not think the Holy Spirit works like that and Jesus appears to have had little use for theology.

The Savior of All Men

Will this decontamination process be entirely successful? Will all humans eventually make it into the new heaven and the new earth? There are certainly some scriptures that imply that:

> *For as in Adam all die, even so in Christ all shall be made alive.*[6]

> *God desires all men to be saved and to come to a knowledge of the truth.*[7]

> *The living God… is the savior of all men, especially those who believe.*[8]

And in a passage that as an Evangelical I used to find doctrinally embarrassing, Peter goes so far as to say that the gospel will be preached to those who have already died, specifically those who were drowned in the Great Flood and who were arguably the most depraved people of all time.[9]

It seems there is a fast track and a slow track into eternity. Those who in this life focus on how they can become perfect, as our heavenly Father is perfect, are like Noah who built an ark to survive the great flood. Those who do not are like the ones who died in the flood. However, Jesus himself goes to them in the afterlife to tell them that although they have died in the flesh they can still be made alive in the spirit.

Will everyone eventually respond to God and make it into the new heaven and the new earth in which righteousness dwells? I do not know. God has built chance and free will into the created universe so maybe even God does not know for certain. Perhaps there will be some who, to adopt Jesus' threefold description, are totally devoid of any sense of justice and have no desire or intention to give up the practicing of lawlessness. These can best be described as sons of the wicked one. Unwilling to change when offered the opportunity or to respond when placed under the most intense pressure they will suffer the wicked one's fate. However, of one thing I am sure; God will stop at nothing until every opportunity to redeem every human has been exhausted. And he has eternity to achieve that.

Too Much Pain

There is one more thing to say to those who are inclined to think that there is too much pain in this whole scenario. Please consider this: God had no experience of pain before he decided to create humans.

God's goal was a fusion between the Creator and the creatures, an intimate friendship, a love affair, an extended family. Angels, wonderful though they are, could never be family in the way that humans can be. However, when you bestow that kind of freedom on an intelligent being the one thing of which you can be absolutely certain is that some if not all of those creatures will seek out and discover all the possible ways to frustrate your intentions. With that comes the experience of pain.

The picture I have in my mind is of God deliberately setting up this universe so that it had the greatest possible capacity for goodness but only at the personal cost to God of exertion, anxiety, frustration and anguish on a vast scale. The point of greatest intensity of pain was the cross. In Jesus the divine and the human melded in a unique way and God experienced the full impact of Jesus' sufferings. God was in Christ reconciling the world to himself. A pathway was opened for all humans and thereby for all creation to enter into the life of God and for God to inhabit the creation.

One of Jesus' parables featured hidden treasure and another spoke about a pearl of great price.[10] In both cases the person making the discovery sold all their possessions in order to acquire these objects of incomparable value. Our salvation has been secured at the price of everything that God possesses. I cannot imagine the extent of what is implied by those words but I can get a hint from the Parable of the Lost Son.[11] In this story Jesus portrays God as a vulnerable and doting father who consents to give one of his sons a large slice of his personal fortune only to see the young man take off to foreign parts, squander all the money and end up destitute. God feels the pain of our alienation and longs for our return.

If you are inclined to think that God's plan entails too much pain then remember that the pearl of great price and the treasure hidden in the field were purchased at Calvary.

Sometimes life feels like an assault course! To build up strength and fitness by training requires effort and discomfort but without pain there is no gain. Either we train in God's way now or we make up with fatigue sessions later! It is far better to be pruned and purged by the Vinedresser now than to be cast later as a fruitless branch into the fire.[12] And anyway that is only God's fallback position; his intention is that we should be made clean by the word of Christ here and now, that we should be trained, like those first disciples were, to become prophetic intercessors who can request and obtain anything from the Father.

If you abide in me, and my words abide in you, you will ask what you desire, and it shall be done for you.

Notes

1. Revelation 12:4,9 cf 1:20
2. Psalm 8:4-6, 1Corinthians 6:3 and Hebrews 1:13,14
3. Matthew 5:48; 2Corinthians 6:18-7:1
4. Matthew13:38,41,49
5. Malachi 3:2,3
6. 1Corinthians 15:22
7. 1Timothy 2:4
8. 1Timothy 4:10
9. 1Peter 3:18-20, 4:5,6 Today's English Version
10. Matthew13:44-46
11. Luke 15:11-32
12. John15:1-17